# The Astrology of Eris

## Pluto's Higher Octave
## Our New Diversity Consciousness

A Dwarf Planet University Publication


Artmedia
4, 101 Britten-Jones Dr
Holt ACT 2615
Australia
www.dwarfplanet.university
alan@artmedia.com.au

The Astrology of Eris
Pluto's Higher Octave
Our New Diversity Consciousness
ISBN: 978-0-6458033-4-1

Cover image by astrologer, Karina La Puma
Author of the series, *A Toolkit for Awakening*
www.soul-source.org

# The Astrology of
# Eris

## Pluto's Higher Octave
## Our New Diversity Consciousness

Alan Clay
Melissa Billington

A Dwarf Planet University Publication

# Contents

## New Stars for a New Era

Many astrologers believe that new planets are discovered when we are ready to incorporate the new consciousness represented by that planet into our existing consciousness. We've noticed this with the discovery of Uranus, Neptune and Pluto over the last two hundred years. And with the discovery of twelve more planets in the past twenty years, we're now entering a period of rapid consciousness development.

Our personal consciousness develops within the collective consciousness around us, and we see this personal consciousness mapped out in the personal planets in our chart. These are the planets out to Saturn that are visible to the naked eye, and they talk about facets of our personality that are important in living day-to-day.

When our consciousness is focussed on the inner planets, everything that is important is our feelings, our ideas and values, our agency and the luck and material rewards that these bring us. "You can't take it with you, right?" And at this level we tend not to be conscious of the action of the outer planets in our lives.

The inner planets represent aspects of personality, while the outer planets represent aspects of consciousness. As each new outer planet is discovered, it represents a new aspect of consciousness that is becoming available to us. The discovery of Uranus brought us intuitive consciousness, the discovery of Neptune, spiritual consciousness, and the discovery of Pluto, psychological consciousness.

So, the discovery of Eris represents a new aspect of consciousness that we can now uncover in ourselves. Put simply, Eris is our new diversity consciousness, teaching us to stop being fooled or to stop fooling ourselves, and to value everyone for who they are. She enables us to find an inner guide, to speak our truth in the world and to embrace our feminine power. However, this new consciousness doesn't kick in automatically, rather we must actively incorporate it into our lives.

Because these outer planets talk of consciousness, how they manifest in our lives depends on our current level of consciousness. Most people on Earth experience the outer planets as unconscious influences and so are unable to be sensitive and adaptable to these esoteric new energies. At this level the outer planets are only perceived when, like Pluto, they barge into our lives in a confrontational way.

As we develop spiritually, however, and consciously on-board these new energies into our lives, they become like guides into new territory, offering us special skills or challenges, depending on the aspects in our chart. At this level, rather than unconscious influences, the outer planets become like a new super-consciousness.

Thus, the discovery of so many new outer planets at one time represents a feast of new consciousness that is now available to us. The enlightenment that was only available to select gurus and priests is now available to everyone. But just as the gurus had to practice devoutly to be able to handle this divine power, we also need to work to on-board these new energies consciously in our lives.

## Physical and Orbital

One of the main ways we discern the meaning of new planets is to look at their physical and orbital characteristics. It tells us a lot about Saturn, that he has 82 moons, 150 moon-like objects, and rings. The precision required for that speaks of his structuring and limiting principals. Uranus spins with East West poles and rotates around the Sun in the opposite direction from most of the other planets, that's very bohemian.

Eris orbits the Sun every 559 years, giving her the greatest orbital period of any of the dwarf planets except for the two sednoids, Sedna and Leleakuhonua. Eris has the largest perspective, encompassing all of the other Kuiper Belt planets in her view. To her, they are all inner planets, but they divide into two different groups which behave quite differently.

All the inner Neptunian planets orbit in a plane around the Sun called the ecliptic, which we can think of as consensus reality. Neptune's gravity and belief systems pull our inner planet energies into a conformity, while all the orbits of the outer dwarf planets cut through this plane at an angle. Eris's orbit is the most highly inclined, at an angle of 44 degrees, which tells us she is going to be much more radical than Pluto, with his pedestrian 17-degree inclination. This inclination gives Eris more perspective, with a higher overview and a deeper *underview* of mainstream reality, which endows her with a greater depth of focus and an x-ray vision that can see through our self-subterfuge.

Eris' orbit is highly eccentric, which is a measure of the elliptical oblongness of her orbit. At the closest point, her perihelion, this brings her inside the orbit of Pluto. She is currently near her furthest point, her aphelion, and she will reach perihelion around the year 2257. This will bring her closer than Pluto currently is, though she never actually crosses Neptune's orbit like he does. This eccentricity tells us that at times Eris' radical spiritual energy will be more present in our world than Pluto's more psychological focus, but it won't get caught up in the Neptunian beliefs and delusions.

Eris is a little smaller than Pluto by area and diameter, but she is 27 percent more massive, which tells us she has a potency that packs more power into a smaller package. She's not fragile like a flower, she's fragile like a bomb. Like a high-powered rifle with a long-range scope, she can both see into and beyond the day-to-day accommodations we make to get by and accurately target the heart of our Neptunian delusional nature.

Eris is far enough from the Sun's heat that methane can condense on her surface, so she appears almost white. This talks of purity and the purification process which is a continual release of what isn't true to arrive at the truth.

Because methane is highly volatile, the Sun's rays should cause a reaction on the surface of the methane ice which would turn it into a red sludge. So, the only way that the surface of Eris can be so white is through a continual renewal of the methane frost on the ice surface. This frost is likely created through a radioactive decay which warms the inner ice mantle, releasing the methane as a gas, and dissipating it to settle on the surface.

Air represents ideas in astrology, so the ice form of the gaseous methane talks of ideas baked into physical form by the actions of time and space. This tells us that Eris enables us to renew our form through a continual dissipation of the intensity of fixed ideas, which creates movement that allows their release. While the volatility suggests that we might get caught up in the argy-bargy of this experience, the frost on the surface suggests a more dispassionate approach.

Eris gives us an ability to continually transmute the volatility we experience, which enables a healthy lifestyle. This is in contrast to the inner explosive power of Pluto which works to dissolve our ego attachments so we can be one with the divine. Pluto rules nuclear power which is a process of releasing the inner power in atoms via radioactive decay. So, Eris's methane dissipation, powered by ongoing radioactive decay, enables us to instead transmute volatility into purity.

Her pure white surface is highly reflective, which makes Eris the brightest planet in our solar system. We associate brightness with intelligence and the ability to perceive what is, as well as shine a light on it. Her brightness encourages full disclosure, which is a theme we will see repeated in the next section on her myth.

Like some of the other dwarf planets, Eris is a binary system with her moon Dysnomia, meaning that they each revolve around a point in the space between them, giving them greater equality. They are tidally locked, always presenting the same face to one another. Binary systems function like a dynamo, translating momentum into energy through their off-centered dynamic interaction. Interestingly, Dysnomia's influence on Eris has been to reduce her spin over time, giving her an increasingly more measured perspective, like the wisdom that can come with age. Dysnomia is one of Eris' children in myth, so we'll explore this dynamic further in the next chapter.

Evidence that Eris has the power to change our perception of the world came as soon as she was discovered, because it led the International Astronomical Union to reclassifying what a planet actually is. Pluto and Ceres were then reclassified as dwarf planets. Officially, a planet must revolve around the Sun, be roughly spherical in shape, and have cleared its orbit. The distinction of the dwarf planets is that they don't clear their orbit, but the Earth also hasn't cleared its orbit, so Earth is also a dwarf planet, and this reminds us that these delineations are arbitrary human constructs.

## Myth

Myths transmit knowledge across time and culture, but they have to be reinterpreted for the new time and the new culture. Eris is the goddess of discord in the Greek and Roman cultures. She is the warrior sister of Mars, and her children are all the products of strife. The siblings are always allied in battle together, but Eris takes no sides in the conflict, laying waste equally to both. She is always the last to leave the battlefield and with each new conflict she rises to the occasion, growing larger until her head brushes the heavens.

The most famous myth of Eris details her role in the Trojan War by triggering the Judgement of Paris. All the other gods and goddesses had been invited to a wedding, along with the rest of Olympus. Chiron did the inviting and he chose to snub Eris because of her troublemaking inclinations. She went anyway and tossed a golden apple into the party, which was inscribed with the phrase, "To the Fairest".

This provoked the goddesses to begin quarreling about who could claim the apple. Paris, the prince of Troy, was appointed by Zeus to resolve the dispute and choose between Hera, Athena, and Aphrodite. Each of the goddesses offered Paris an inducement – Hera promised him land and riches, Athena promised victory in battle, and Aphrodite the love of the most beautiful woman in the world, Queen Helen of Sparta. He chose Aphrodite, and the subsequent abduction of Helen led directly to the Trojan War and the eventual fall of the city of Troy.

We can see the themes of this myth are inclusion verses exclusion, and competition based on self-image, personal vanity, and the judgments we make of others. These judgements lead to us pushing others down in order to win material reward and recognition. Discord and war inevitably ensue from this competition, which is the origin of Eris' reputation as the Goddess of Discord.

But Eris doesn't cause the strife, she just reveals it by throwing the golden apple into the gathering, which encourages it, so that the strife can be dealt with and we can live in harmony. Or if she does cause the strife, it is the necessary spark to activate our will to recognise and engage with what we've been ignoring or denying. At the spiritual level, Eris is promoting a diversity consciousness which wants everyone to be included and no-one to be judged.

It's interesting that Chiron was in charge of the wedding invitations. Chiron is always encouraging our growth, frequently by appearing to damage us in some way, and, in the healing that ensues, we grow. In his choice not to invite Eris, Chiron played a similar role in the myth, triggering Eris to provoke the growth of her diversity consciousness amongst the gods with her provocative apple. Chiron invited this new consciousness into our world by not inviting Eris to the wedding.

Modern research on this myth has actually brought to light that Zeus was plotting to start the war before the wedding snub, for which Eris was conveniently made the fall girl. Often, those of us with a strong Eris have been demonized for speaking out about the underlying truth we perceive. Or we have learned to mask our innate power just to survive consensus reality.

In the myth, with each new conflict Eris grew larger until her head brushed the heavens, so she gives us the power we need to bravely deal with any disharmony that we encounter. When we fail to address the underlying causes of conflict and strife, however, they will grow larger until an intervention from heaven is needed to resolve the issues.

These new outer planets represent new aspects of consciousness that are becoming available to us, and how they manifest in our lives depends on our current level of consciousness. The myths tell us about the unconscious influence, because that's how people were when the myth was developed, and most people on the planet today are unconscious of these new energies.

We're often racing after the golden apple in our mortal lives, and we can see that the strife and material competition associated with Eris are going to be particularly apparent at the unconscious level. When we're unconscious of Eris, she manifests as discord and strife externally in our interactions with others and also internally in our thoughts and motivations. We are often fighting with ourselves through our contradictory desires and beliefs. So, learning to be tolerant within ourselves, to not feel torn apart by seemingly contradictory aspects of ourselves promotes a healthy body and a healthy mind.

At this unconscious level, Eris is always motivating us to compete with one another and push others down in the process. However, as we embrace a more spiritual understanding and develop our diversity consciousness, we see that, in fact, there is no competition. Everyone has their unique value, and we recognize that we don't need to push others down to pull ourselves up. We all have a right to exist, because we all do exist.

Once we are on the spiritual path, the myth suggests that Eris enables us to see clearly without preconceptions and helps us keep our body and mind in harmony so that health and happiness prevail. Because of the depth and x-ray vision with Eris, at the spiritual level we become adept at diplomatically navigating our interactions with others and engaging at the appropriate level with each person.

At the spiritually evolved level Eris is a truth-telling trickster, like the sacred fools of the Sufi tradition who are the revered teachers. The Sufi teachers traveled from village to village, playing the role of the fool, able to talk to anybody and say just what was needed to that person at that time to assist their spiritual evolution. At the highest level, Eris enables this in us. We learn to see what people are ready to accept and are able to offer the spiritual nudge they need.

## Reimagining the Mars Archetype

Eris is the warrior sister of Mars. However, seeing her only as a sister, limits our perception of her innate power and our ability to embrace this archetype. New planets are discovered when we are ready to incorporate the energies they represent, so we are now at the point where we have the power to reimagine the Mars archetype. Mars is a product of the paternalistic paradigm that we are evolving out of, and our reinterpretation of Eris gives us a new relationship with anger and conflict.

Because we're evolving out of the paternalistic paradigm, we imagine that it has always been this way. We forget that we had an extended period of matriarchal culture before that, which was Venus based, centered in arts, community, and nature-connection. However, the Mars archetype is inherent in our evolution from nature-based cultures to the modern-day. So, we are in a period of reimagining the Mars archetype and the role of men in today's world through his sister's higher consciousness.

While Eris played the warrior sister to Mars, she took no sides in the battle, laying waste equally to both. Her problem is the battle itself. As we embrace our diversity consciousness, we learn to allow the opposing point of view so that there is no battle. There is only conflict when we feel challenged by others believing differently than we do. When we can allow others to believe what they believe, there is no conflict and we achieve harmony.

Belief is a Neptunian construct, and we saw in the orbital section that Eris's orbit does not cross that of Neptune, which enables this plurality. The way we are revealing Eris here is an example of plurality in action. We are reinterpreting the older Mars myth as a fractal of the new diversity consciousness itself. We don't deny or refute the old or existing views, but instead allow them to stand side by side, giving you the choice of what best empowers your evolving consciousness.

Where Mars is a fractal that gives us access to the bigger Erisian view, Eris can be seen as a hologram of Mars. A hologram uses a laser beam of coherent light to clarify a chaotic pattern into a clear representation of a 3D object. Viewed under normal light, the pattern looks chaotic, but the laser beam defines it clearly. In the myth, the golden apple becomes the object that illuminates the pattern of competition between the goddesses. Similarly, Eris's laser focus in our lives points to the disharmony that we need to address to reach harmony. So, her higher consciousness and clear perception is a repolarization of Mars' energy, which is what we are in dire need of today.

## Eris' Children

Eris has many children and they are all the products of discord, such as back-breaking toil, forgetfulness, starvation, lawlessness, and ruin. It's notable that discord and strife breed rapidly. When we're not attuned to the underlying disharmony, it breeds rapidly, showing up in our work as back-breaking toil, in our health as starvation, and in our governments as the breakdown of civil order, for only a few examples.

One of Eris' daughters, Dysnomia, which Eris' moon was named after, personifies lawlessness and the breakdown of civil order. Because the moon rotates around the planet, Dysnomia provides an environment of lawlessness and civil disorder in which Eris operates. The interaction between them refines her clear focus on what needs to be resolved. As we explored in the orbital characteristics, astronomically, Dysnomia has slowed Eris's spin over time. So, the disorder in our environment slows the spin of our diversity consciousness and over time this gives us a wisdom that comes from experience.

## Sabian Symbol for the Discovery Degree

The Sabian Symbols were channelled by clairvoyant Elsie Wheeler and astrologer Marc Edmund Jones, and they give us rich visual symbols for each degree of the zodiac. We can look at the degree of Eris in her discovery chart like a birth moment. As the new planet arrives in our consciousness, the Sabian Symbol of that degree gives us another way to understand the meaning of the planet. We'll look at the discovery chart as a whole in a coming chapter but first let's explore the Sabian Symbol for Eris' placement in that chart.

Eris was discovered at 19 degrees 45 minutes of Aries, and we round this up to find the Sabian Symbol. So, the symbol for 20 degrees Aries is:

**A Young Girl Feeding Birds in Winter**

Let's look at interpretations for this symbol from three respected astrologers, and remember, as we read them, that these are interpretations of Eris. Firstly, from Dane Rudhyar.

> *KEYNOTE:* ***Overcoming crises through compassion.***
> *Migrating birds fly south, but by establishing a partnership with other creatures unable to escape wintry deprivation or death, Man can maintain the life of the spirit - symbolized by birds - steady through all crises if, like a "young girl," he is widely open to the promptings of love and sympathy. The theme is: The Transmutation of Life into Love.*[1]

Transmutation implies transforming into a higher element, so this symbol tells us that when we encounter discord in our lives, Eris is providing us with an opportunity to transmute that experience into love. Despite her reputation as the Goddess of Discord, she gives us the ability to be 'steady through all crises' and to solve these crises through love and compassion.

By being open to others, we nourish the spiritual part of our lives, which enables our ability to fly, to soar above everything. When we widen our gaze to the full picture, which echoes the large orbit of Eris, we're not caught up in the day-to-day discord. It's notable that the unarmoured nature of innocence opens us to 'the promptings of love and sympathy' and enables us to 'maintain the life of the spirit'.

---

1 Dane Rudhyar, An Astrological Mandala,

James Burgess sees this symbol as:

> *Seeing life as a constant opportunity to experience love and being innocent and fearless in that love. Life's very harshness is what enables us to learn of love's unfathomable depth. Nature is harsh – people and animals suffer and starve, and they die. Yet without harshness compassion could not exist; there would be no place for it. There is no higher purpose than to live life as a constant expression of compassionate love. This is neither fanciful nor sentimental love; it is feeding the hungry stranger.*[2]

Eris brings us the ability to love fearlessly, a love that enables us to stand up for ourselves and others and do the real compassionate work required to enable it. She brings a profound lesson in selfless compassion, in overcoming harsh realities by expressing innocent love, and in nurturing spiritual sustenance even in barren times. She enables us to move beyond sentimental feelings to true, active care for others' essential needs.

And Lynda Hill says:

> *This symbol shows the ability to help those in need of help, to provide safety, security, nourishment or emotional support, especially to those who may not know how to solve their problems themselves. There are those that stubbornly resist moving on or changing their habits, even if it is to their detriment, and providing them with a safe harbor can bring many rewards. This is about sharing and caring. Non-judgmental attitudes can move you to help them and lead them to trust. A dedication to helping others has its own rewards. However, be careful of trying to win approval, co-dependent relationships, lack of boundaries and feeling used.*[3]

When we embrace Eris's energy at the spiritual level, she encourages us to care for others who are working at a more unconscious level and who are unable to solve their problems themselves. Rather than lifting others' consciousness through the argy-bargy of the interactions, simply providing them a safe harbor enables them to grow in consciousness.

Similarly, we often get on our high horse about our beliefs and judge others or try to win approval by playing into others' beliefs and expectations.

---

2 www.jamesburgess.com/a-young-girl-feeding-birds-in-winter.html
3 www.sabiansymbols.com

Our perception of their evolutionary path can get in the way of enabling them to follow it. Letting go of the perceived reward of being the teacher allows us to be present for what the other truly needs.

## Eris as a Higher Octave

Another way of understanding these new outer planets is to look at them as a higher octave of an inner planet that we know well. The higher octave expresses the inner energy at a more spiritual level. However, the inner planet is not only stepped up to a higher level, its energy is also repolarized by the higher octave. This enables a more spiritual expression of that inner energy in our daily lives.

When Pluto was discovered, one way of understanding him was as the higher octave of Mars, lifting the active battling energy of Mars into the transformative power of Pluto. And because of Eris' sisterly bond with Mars in myth, we propose that Eris is the higher octave of Pluto. Lifting his transformative psychological energy into a fierce grace that blesses our lives with divine power. All three planets have assertive and transformative qualities.

As we know, Mars enables us to go about getting what we want in the world. He is the essential fire we need to be embodied. These days Mars has a bad reputation from his warlike nature, but as we explored in the myth, since the discovery of Pluto we have been reimagining the application of this vital energy in our lives.

Over the past hundred years since his discovery, Pluto has been repolarizing Mars' warrior energy, transforming his assertiveness into a more spiritual level of application. We've seen this in the growth and development of Pluto's psychological consciousness over this time, reinterpreting the Martian ego impulses through this new understanding. The advent of the nuclear threat and the growing awareness of ecocide and ongoing genocides, is a product of the unconscious level of Pluto, and this is forcing us to rethink the application of Mars' warrior energy. Most of us only grow when we have to do so to survive, and that's what these existential threats are pushing us to do.

As the higher octave of Pluto, Eris is a truth-telling activist who is repolarizing his transformative energy into a brave capacity to confront our own foolishness. She takes Pluto's dynamic and dark reputation and sees the value in his shadow and his embrace of the natural lifecycle, including death. This new vision enables us to re-see our relationship with the dark. Eris repolarizes Pluto's focus on death and dying by giving us a bigger soul view that transcends the battles of this lifetime.

Where Mars fights mundane enemies, Eris is working to free us through esoteric confrontations, where we have to stop being fooled, or stop fooling ourselves.

Eris transforms Pluto's male power into an inclusive female power that transmutes life into love. Where the assertiveness of Mars and Pluto is forceful, Eris' strength is in her sensitive humility. As we develop spiritually, we learn not to put ourselves over others and we can engage with them at the level required to facilitate what's needed in each moment. Eris gives us the strength to resist the mainstream and stick to truth no matter how humbling. In this light, it's significant that her discovery repolarized Pluto in our consciousness by shifting his status from planet to dwarf planet.

**Higher Octave Case Study – Alice Bailey**

Now, if these three planets are octaves of one another, we would expect to find them singing in chorus in major events in our lives. Let's examine these three octaves in the chart of the influential esoteric writer and teacher, Alice Bailey, when she founded her Arcane School. We'll look at Alice in more depth a little later, but for now let's look at the action of Mars, Pluto and Eris as she started her famous school. Alice coined the term New Age, so the start of her school can be seen as the birth of the New Age Movement.

She was born in 1880 and grew up in a wealthy middle class British family, receiving an Anglican education, before becoming a devoted missionary worker and Sunday school teacher. When she was 35 she joined the Theosophical Society and began to study *Blavatsky's Secret Doctrines*. A few years later, a spirit guide came to her who identified himself as a Tibetan master called Djwhal Khul. She then wrote a series of 'ageless wisdom books' which she described as his teachings.

Let's start by looking at the placements of these three octaves in her natal chart. She has Mars conjunct her Ascendant, in a close quintile with her Pluto in the 10$^{th}$ house of occupation, which in turn is in a close quintile with her Eris in the 8$^{th}$ house of the occult. Mars and Eris are therefore in a close biquintile, so the three octaves are strongly aligned with evolutionary flows in her chart.

At the unconscious level, an 8$^{th}$ house Eris can encourage materialist greed, an interest in kinky sex, and a desire to sow chaos in the

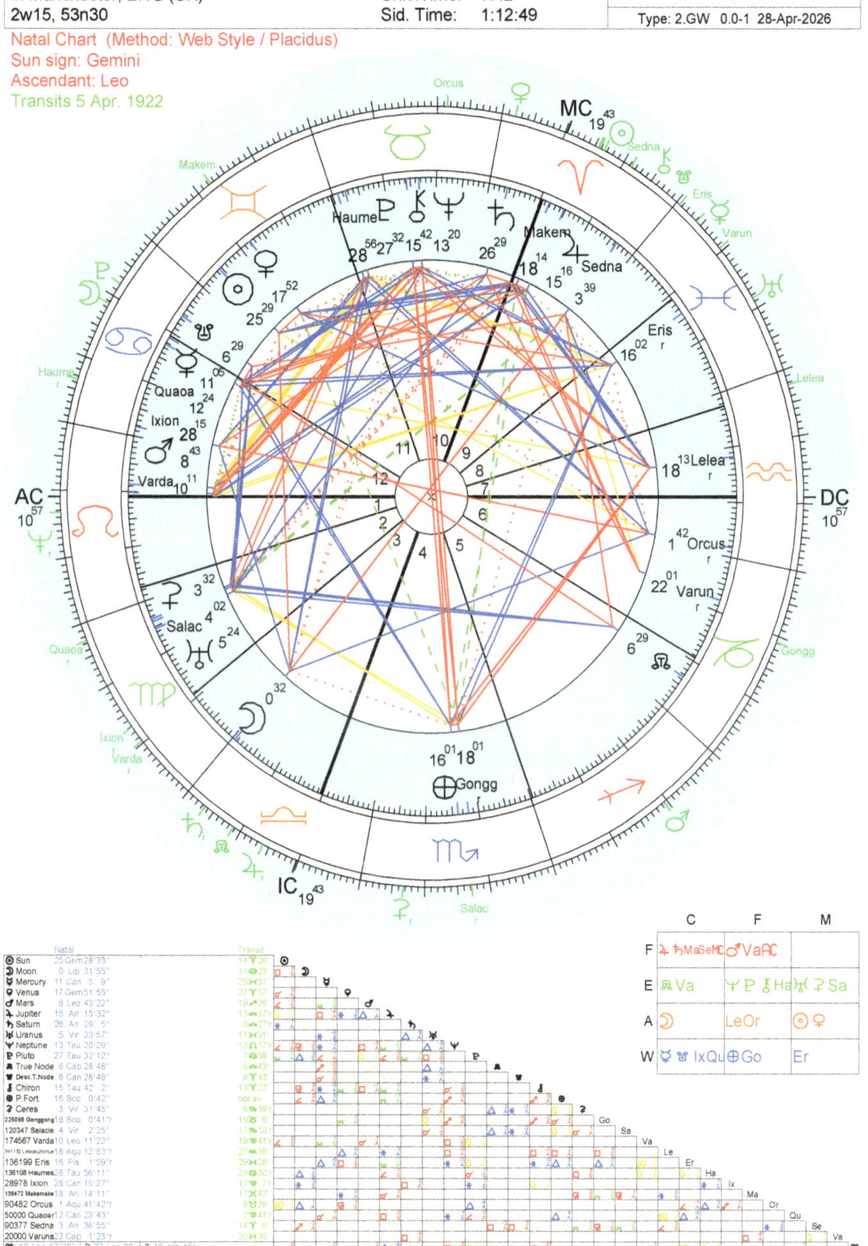

Name: ♀ Alice A. Bailey [Adb]
born on We., 16 June 1880
in Manchester, ENG (UK)
2w15, 53n30
Time: 7:42 a.m.
Univ.Time: 7:42
Sid. Time: 1:12:49
ASTRO DIENST
www.astro.com
Type: 2.GW 0.0-1 28-Apr-2026
Natal Chart (Method: Web Style / Placidus)
Sun sign: Gemini
Ascendant: Leo
Transits 5 Apr. 1922
MC 19 43
AC 10 57
DC 10 57
IC 19 43
Haumea
Makem
Sedna
Eris
Lelea
Orcus
Varun
Gongg
Salac
Quaoa
Ixion
Varda
Natal
Transit
Sun 25 Gem 28'33"
Moon 0 Lib 31'55"
Mercury 11 Can 5' 9"
Venus 17 Gem 51'53"
Mars 8 Leo 43'22"
Jupiter 15 Ari 15'32"
Saturn 26 Ari 29' 5"
Uranus 5 Vir 23'57"
Neptune 13 Tau 20'29"
Pluto 27 Tau 32'12"
True Node 6 Cap 28'48"
Desc.T.Node 6 Can 28'48"
Chiron 15 Tau 42' 2"
P.Fort. 16 Sco 0'42"
Ceres 3 Vir 31'45"
225088 Gonggong 18 Sco 0'41"r
120347 Salacia 4 Vir 2'25"
174567 Varda 10 Leo 11'22"
541132 Leleakuhonua 18 Aqu 12'53"r
136199 Eris 16 Pis 1'59"r
136108 Haumea 28 Tau 56'11"
28978 Ixion 28 Can 15'27"
136472 Makemake 18 Ari 14'11"
90482 Orcus 1 Aqu 41'42"r
50000 Quaoar 12 Can 23'43"
90377 Sedna 3 Ari 38'55"
20000 Varuna 22 Cap 1'23"r
AC: 10 Leo 57'20"
2: 27 Leo 29'
3: 19 Vir 15'
MC: 19 Ari 43'17"
11: 0 Gem 20'
12: 10 Can 39'
C F M
F E A W

collective energies. However, we see in this study that the spiritually evolved level Eris in the 8th house is in touch with deep truths and can bring them into our world. In so doing, she fosters our collective energies and has the power to enliven them and inspire new faith.

Alice established the Lucis Trust, which ran her Arcane School, on the 5th April 1922. It was established "as a vehicle to foster recognition of the universal spiritual principles at the heart of all work to build right relations". On that day, she had transiting Eris in the 9th house of belief and higher education, sextile her natal Pluto in the 10th within 1 degree. At the highest level, Pluto in the 10th is working with social transformation, and the 'occult guidance' from her natal Eris in the 8th gave form to that in the school.

We don't tend to think of dwarf planet Pluto as spiritual because we tend to experience his energy at the unconscious level, but just like the other dwarfs, he manifests differently depending on our consciousness level. At the highest level, Pluto in the 10th isn't into power in our normal sense of the word, but rather a spiritual power so strong it can effect social transformation. It is a bit like a fierce grace, but only a bit, because this is a term we reserve for Eris at the highest level.

That day Alice had Pluto transiting through the 11th house of collective consciousness, closely semi-sextile her natal Mars, which is conjunct her Ascendant. So, her transformative consciousness mission was flowing with her actions and behavior. Again, we see the three octaves working together in these transits. Mars, meanwhile, was transiting through her 5th house, closely trine her Midheaven and closely biquintile her Neptune in the 10th, so her actions that day were flowing with her place in society and were in an evolutionary flow with her spiritual vision and her occupation.

As well as the sextile to Pluto, transiting Eris was also opposite her Moon, within one degree, and square her Sun, within three degrees. We see here the importance of the event in these aspects to the lights in her chart. But the closest aspect Eris is making is a sextile to her natal Haumea on the 11th house cusp. Haumea represents rebirth, so the sextile talks about the rebirth of collective consciousness that occurred through the school.

As well as the semi-sextile to Mars, transiting Pluto was closely quintile her natal Saturn in the 10th, giving her teaching a new structure and taking it to a new evolutionary level. Pluto was also conjunct her South Node in the $11^{th}$ house, within one degree, transforming her karmic power in the collective consciousness and setting up her destiny with the opposition to the North Node. So, we do see the resonance of the three octaves working together in this event.

A year after it was established, the trust published her 'great invocation prayer', which became very popular. The trust went on to publish 24 books in 50 languages. The harmony of all three octaves in her natal chart gave her a spiritual fire that, more than a century later, means that Alice's writing continues to strongly influence those interested in the occult and in deep spiritual mysteries. This influence shows us how at the top level the humble female power of Eris is able to connect appropriately with each person to facilitate their individual spiritual growth.

## Discovery Chart Interpretation

Another way that we can understand these new planets is to look at the chart for the planet's discovery. In her discovery chart, Eris is the leading planet in the 1st House, the house of identity, which gives her energy a centered quality that counterbalances her all-encompassing embrace. She has the focus to be present in the moment and do whatever is needed. This enlightened self-centeredness is why she rules on the battlefield, and it gives us the surgical cutting-through power to show up in our lives with a fierce grace that enables us to take action on the important matters.

Her chart has a compassionate flavor to it and the main expression of this is her Moon conjunct Ceres in Scorpio in the 7th House. Moon in Scorpio is emotionally very sensitive and aware of the power dynamics that are underlying our outward behavior. And Ceres brings a sensitivity to the give and take of love in these power dynamics, and she can bring about a change in the balance of power. So, Eris wants there to be an even give and take of love in our interactions, and from this seat of nurturance we can rebalance the power dynamics.

The 7th House focuses these power dynamics in our one-to-one relationships. And we can see from this Ceres-Moon conjunction in this house that, as we develop our new diversity consciousness, Eris gives us the ability to connect with each person at their own level by being sensitive to who they are.

The conjunction of Ceres and the Moon is in a grand water trine with Salacia, our new planet of higher-love consciousness, in Pisces in the 12th house, and Varuna, our new planet of mastery consciousness, in Cancer in the 4th house. We can think of Salacia as the higher octave of Venus and Mars combined, so she's all about the psychic contact we have in our intimate relationships. In the 12th House, Salacia is mediating an intimate connection with the masses on an unconscious level. So, Eris enables us to feel the vibes on the battlefield of life and connect intimately with each of the combatants.

And the Moon-Ceres trine with Varuna in the 4th is enabling our new mastery consciousness with that sensitivity, which enhances Eris' ability to nurture. We can look at Varuna as being the higher octave of Saturn, giving his structure more personal sovereignty. However Varuna's sovereignty is gained through experience, which is what gives

| Name: Eris Discovery | | |
|---|---|---|
| date: We., 5 January 2005 | Time: | 11:20 a.m. |
| in Pasadena, CA (US) | Univ.Time: | 19:20 |
| 118w09, 34n09 | Sid. Time: | 18:29:19 |

Type: 2.GW 0.0-1 28-Apr-2026

Event Chart (Method: Web Style / Placidus)
Sun sign: Capricorn
Ascendant: Aries

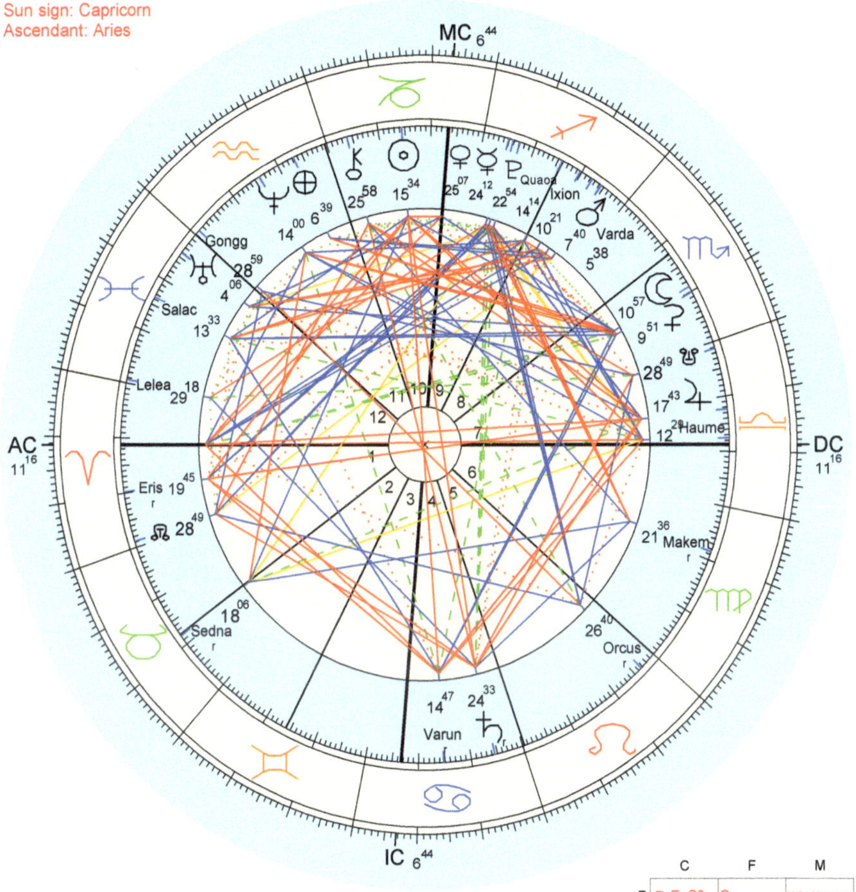

|  |  |
|---|---|
| ☉ Sun | 15 Cap 33'51" |
| ☽ Moon | 10 Sco 56'59" |
| ☿ Mercury | 24 Sag 11'48" |
| ♀ Venus | 25 Sag 8'56" |
| ♂ Mars | 7 Sag 39'55" |
| ♃ Jupiter | 17 Lib 42'50" |
| ♄ Saturn | 24 Can 32'50"r |
| ♅ Uranus | 4 Pis 6'30" |
| ♆ Neptune | 14 Aqu 0'30" |
| ♇ Pluto | 22 Sag 53'47" |
| ☊ True Node | 28 Ari 48'52" |
| ☋ Desc.T.Node | 28 Lib 48'52" |
| ⚷ Chiron | 25 Cap 58' 8" |
| ⊕ P.Fort. | 6 Aqu 39'27" |
| ⚳ Ceres | 9 Sco 51'23" |
| 225088 Gonggong | 28 Aqu 58'40" |
| 120347 Salacia | 13 Pis 32'37" |
| 174567 Varda | 5 Sag 37'57" |
| 541132 Leleakuhonua | 29 Pis 18'13" |
| 136199 Eris | 19 Ari 45'22"r |
| 136108 Haumea | 12 Lib 29' 0" |
| 28978 Ixion | 10 Sag 20'31" |
| 136472 Makemake | 21 Vir 36' 6"r |
| 90482 Orcus | 26 Leo 39'47"r |
| 50000 Quaoar | 14 Sag 13'56" |
| 90377 Sedna | 18 Tau 6'30"r |
| 20000 Varuna | 14 Can 47' 3"r |

| AC: 11 Ari 16'19" | 2: 17 Tau 51' | 3: 14 Gem 7' |
|---|---|---|
| MC: 6 Cap 43'52" | 11: 0 Aqu 21' | 12: 29 Aqu 57' |

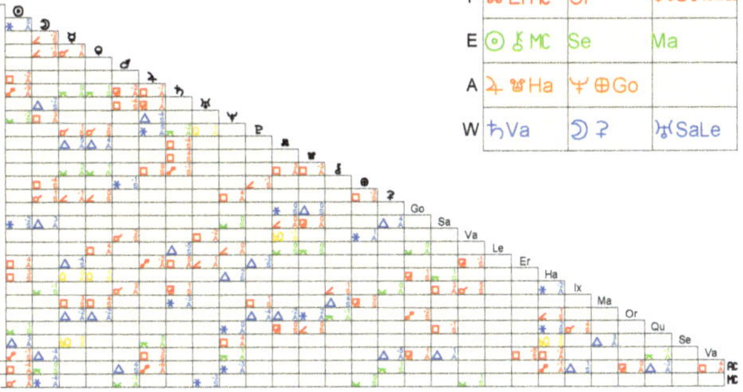

| | C | F | M |
|---|---|---|---|
| F | ☊ Er AC | Or | ☿♀♂♇ Va Ix Qu |
| E | ☉ ⚷ MC | Se | Ma |
| A | ♃ ☋ Ha | ♆ ⊕ Go | |
| W | ♄ Va | ☽ ⚳ | ♅ Sa Le |

us the mastery, and it is not dependent on approval or permission in the same way as it is with Saturn. So, this grand trine in Eris' discovery chart gives us a psychic ability to ground mastery in our one-to-one relationships when we embrace her compassionate power.

The compassionate nature of Eris' energy is reinforced by the placements of Saturn and Varuna in Cancer in the 4th House. We see from this that Eris' lessons are delivered from compassion, but we may not perceive them that way. Eris' truth nurtures us in the long run, even if it can be hard to hear at the start. The house placement of Saturn and Varuna, opposite her Sun in the 10th, emphasizes the need to make a sacred space to ground Eris' transformative power. As we do this, we embrace her diversity consciousness, enabling the uplift of our own consciousness.

The 10th House Sun in Capricorn gives her energy a practical and social emphasis that trusts the longer journey, and so she is determined to work moment by moment to reach her goal. Chiron is also in the 10th House, reflecting the way Eris is misunderstood and the way we often feel wounded by the directness of her actions in our lives. Wounding-and-healing is a growth process, so as we grow we come to revalue our wounds as the necessary experiences to evolve and learn to see them as blessings in disguise. Just as we strengthen our physical muscles in a tear-and-repair process, Eris' actions in our lives strengthens our soul muscle. The more we embrace Eris' energy and trust the longer journey, the more we grow from each encounter and the less challenging Eris is.

Pluto, Mercury, and Venus are all in bed together in the 9th House in Sagittarius. This sign placement indicates that Eris has our highest interest at heart in the exercise of her transformative power. This stellium is talking about the cutting ability that Eris has in her relationships and communications to transform and empower us (insert Evil Laugh!). In a normal person's chart, this combination of the transformative power of Pluto's psychological consciousness with the inner planets would be problematic, contentious, and challenging. But in a goddess's chart we see how the power of her Pluto is coupled with the kindness of her Venus and the curiosity of her Mercury. This says that Eris' energy manifests intimately in the world. She's right there with us in our communications and valued connections, whether we're aware of her or not.

This Sagittarius stellium forms one of the three corners of a grand fire trine. The other two are her North Node in Aries, at the anaretic degree in the 1st House, and Orcus in Leo in the 5th House. Orcus is our new karmic consciousness who at the top level gives us an ability to transmute shadow into light. This is creatively expressed in the 5th House. And the North Node in Aries has the capacity to create new karma, which enables us to escape old patterns. As we adopt a more spiritual expression, this grand trine means that Eris empowers us to deal creatively with the shadow we encounter and transmute it into the light that sustains us. And the 9th house placement of the stellium tells us that the more philosophically we can view the confrontations Eris brings us, the more we will benefit from her wisdom.

Pluto is the lower octave of Eris, so let's look at the harmony with his lower octave, Mars, which is in the 8th House, also in Sagittarius, and conjunct Varda and Ixion. Varda is our new inspiration consciousness, which enables us to shine our light in the world or to find the light in the darkness, and to win the battles in our lives through hope and inspiration. Ixion is our seeker consciousness, enabling us to be authentic and to follow our bliss. So, this stellium gives Eris a hopeful authentic action that's plugged into the deeper mysteries.

It is interesting that the two lower octaves are both in the fire sign of Sagittarius, Mars towards the beginning and Pluto towards the end, while Eris is in the first fire sign, Aries. Aries is about living the myth, and Sagittarius philosophizes on the wider picture. So, the higher octave in Aries gives Eris's expression in our lives an innocence and creates the opportunity for a fresh start. In the 8th and 9th houses, the two lower octaves are gathering in the collective baggage and philosophies, but with the higher octave in the 1st there's a dynamic activation of her purity. This tells us that when we activate the three octaves, Eris gives us the power to live on a mythic level—as though she's saying, "Let's go out and do this stuff guys!"

Our new planet of unity consciousness, Haumea, is conjunct the Descendant in the 7th House in Libra. Haumea is the Hawaiian goddess of rebirth who connects us to the oneness of our experience, to the magic of being alive, and this connection brings rejuvenation into our lives. The conjunction with the Descendent tells us that there is a regenerative power in each of the intimate transformative connections that Eris enables us to make with the world. Our lives are reformed by each. The opposition to the Ascendant means that we can successfully mediate this creative possibility in each moment by embracing the higher consciousness of Eris. It's through the regenerative psychic connection in each relationship that we see Eris' female power expressed.

Haumea in Libra is into human rights and social justice, or, at a lower level, a holiday in the Bahamas, and the opposition to the Ascendant infuses this into Eris' influence on our behavior. When we find ourselves relating to life in a lower-level Erisian way, we need to tune into the through-lines that connect us to knowing, trusting, and doing what's right. We first need to recognize that we're in the lower-level expression in order to activate Eris' wisdom and then we have the potential to rebirth instantaneously. The true warrior's path lies in letting go of the battles and the baggage.

Having the angles in cardinal signs, with her Sun in Capricorn and her Ascendant in Aries, creates a strong initiatory energy in her chart. Eris is known mythologically as the Goddess of Discord, which is how we experience this cardinal energy when we're not open to the necessary change of season. We actually need discord in our lives to grow. Change only occurs in the to-and-fro of discord. You might think that the Sun in Capricorn in the $10^{th}$ house makes her prone to maintaining the establishment, but she's a spiritual trickster so it is her nature and role in our lives is to disrupt the status quo.

And one final point, we're seeing a sharpness in Eris' energy throughout this interpretation which is an important part of the awakening consciousness she brings to us. No one cuddles up to the alarm.

## Astrological Meaning

So, let's pull this together. Eris enables our diversity consciousness as we learn to value everything and everyone for who they truly are. She encourages us to simultaneously see ourselves in an uncompromising way and also to be inclusive in our world view. We tend to fool ourselves and overlook our shortcomings just to get through each day, but Eris draws her strength from the unflinching nature of her understanding. It's all valuable to her and we'll only be complete and embrace our full power when we adopt a practice of full disclosure and accept our multifaceted nature.

Similarly, in the outer world, Eris wants everyone to be valued and included. And she has no time for judgment or comparison. She teaches us to maintain a steady spirit through all crises by being open to the promptings of love and sympathy. This is vital for our spiritual growth because it gives us the strength and courage necessary to take the spiritual risks required. It encourages us to develop an open heart, which is essential for personal transformation and expanded consciousness. Our lives go through different phases, but through compassion we are able to support ourselves and one another through any challenge: and by facing the challenge we learn to transmute that effort into love.

From the mythology we know that she encourages us to rise to any challenge and to stand our ground until we are the last warrior on the battlefield. But, while this tenaciousness can be a great benefit, we don't always need to slay everyone else to make our point. We have to understand when we have already won, and when to leave well enough alone.

In our personal lives, her laser focus points to the disharmony that we need to address to reach an internal harmony. When we're not attuned to the underlying disharmony, it breeds rapidly, but Eris gives us the ability to be present in the moment, and the power to bravely deal with any disharmony we encounter. This enlightened self-centeredness is why she rules on the battlefield, and it gives us the surgical cutting-through power to show up in our lives with a fierce grace that enables us to take action on the important matters.

As we've seen, we are in a period of reimagining the Mars archetype and the role of men in today's world through his sister's higher diversity consciousness. Where Mars is fighting mundane battles, Eris' challenge is on a more esoteric level, bringing battles that open us to our divine fulfillment as we transmute them into love. In modern astrology Pluto is considered to be the higher octave of Mars, so we can look at Eris as the higher octave of Pluto. She steps up his transformative energy to a fierce grace through which everything in our lives is opened to the light and can be transmuted into love.

If we are still at the personal planet level of consciousness, however, and sensing this influence unconsciously, we are likely to get caught up in the battles in our lives. Or we might actively seek them out by getting on our high horse about what is important for us, or by speaking out about something, whether this is appropriate or not. These confrontations shine light on parts of ourselves that we have denied or pushed into the unconscious or simply taken for granted. We need discord to grow. It's only in the to-and-fro of opposing points of view that change occurs. Eris doesn't really cause trouble; she just shines a light on the need for change by provoking our natural reactions so we can see where they lead. At this level, Eris is teaching us to stop being fooled, or to stop fooling ourselves.

At the same time, she is also likely encouraging us to be competitive, and to take any advantage when we can, because 'everyone else does!'. When we buy into the rampant greed and selfishness of the capitalist system, it convinces us that there is no other way - that the rat race is the only game in town, so we join it with Eris' whole-heartedness. Or we might go to any lengths to be included in some enterprise or social group, compromising ourselves in the process. Or we could be unable to compromise and so not allowed to participate. As a result, we may feel alienated and excluded from meaningful social interaction.

When we find ourselves relating to life in this lower-level Erisian way, we need to tune into the through-lines that connect us to knowing, trusting, and doing what's right. We first need to recognize that we're in the lower-level expression in order to activate Eris's wisdom and then we have the potential for instantaneous rebirth. By realising that the true warrior's path lies in letting go of the battles and the baggage, and learning to view the confrontations she brings us philosophically, we gain the benefit of her wisdom.

We often feel wounded by the directness of Eris' actions in our lives. Wounding-and-healing is a growth process, so as we grow we come to revalue our wounds as necessary experiences to evolve and see them as blessings in disguise. Just as we strengthen our physical muscles in a tear-and-repair process, Eris's actions in our lives strengthens our soul muscle. The more we embrace her energy and trust the longer journey, the more we grow from each encounter and the less challenging she is.

As we develop spiritually, she gives us a depth of focus and an x-ray vision that enables us to see through our own self-subterfuge. Like a high-powered rifle with a long-range scope, she enables us to both see into and beyond the day-to-day accommodations we make to get by and accurately target the heart of our delusional nature.

We learn that our strife can be dealt with simply by accepting the opposing point of view, and that without strife, we can live in harmony. This diversity consciousness enables us to understand that the problem is seeing the opposing view as a challenge. To accept an opposing view, we have to grow spiritually, so that our belief is not challenged by the lack of the same belief in another. At this level, Eris becomes the goddess of pluralism, enabling us each to believe what works for us.

As we develop this spiritual approach, we can embrace a practice of love and compassion. We realize that growing spiritually and pushing the boundaries of our understanding is challenging and uncertain, requiring a willingness to step out of our comfort zone and face potential obstacles and we know that love and compassion gives us the motivation and support we need to navigate these risks.

Learning to be tolerant within ourselves, to not feel torn apart by seemingly contradictory aspects of ourselves, promotes a healthy body and a healthy mind. Likewise in the outer world, as we learn to see clearly without preconceptions, it also helps us to keep our body and mind in harmony so that health and happiness prevail. The mischief or misbehavior that we indulged in at the unconscious level, is clearly off limits now that we see our lives in a higher light.

While at the unconscious level those of us with a strong Eris have frequently been demonized for speaking out about the underlying truth we perceive, at the spiritual level we become adept at diplomatically navigating our interactions with others and engaging at the appropriate level with each person. We learn to see what people are ready to see and are able to offer the spiritual nudge they need.

At the top level, we understand Eris' fierce grace for the transmuted love that it is. We know that it is through engaging and doing the work that this effort is transmuted into love. And this gives us a female power that we can bring to bear in our lives. Where the male power of Pluto and Mars is frequently coercive, Eris' power is more sensitive and gentle in its engagement, but it rises to meet the needs of any challenge.

Eris gives us the power to change our perception of the world, which enables us to transmute the volatility of our experience into the purity of wisdom. Like the planet herself, as we reduce the spin in our lives we gain an increasingly measured perspective. This purification process, which is a continual release of what isn't true to arrive at the truth, is the wisdom that comes with age.

When we embrace her fierce grace, Eris brings a sacred wisdom into our lives. This may manifest as a spirit guide who can help us with sacred knowledge. Or as a connection to our inner guide, the part of us that knows where we are in our dance between karma and dharma, and what is best in each situation. At this level, we become a truth-telling trickster, able to get our message through by crafting it perfectly for each person. We value everyone as they are, accepting everything and neither comparing nor judging.

## Too Hot to Handle

Eris brings sacred truth into our lives, and we have to be ready to 'handle it', or we will blow a fuse. Just like the yogis of old who practiced devoutly to be able to channel divine grace, work is required to enable and integrate these new outer planet energies. We do the work by learning to ground Eris' light in practical ways in our daily lives.

When we're not ready to do this, we are likely to project it outwards and tell everyone else what they should do. It is all too easy to see what others should do with their lives, but much harder to turn that transpersonal gaze on ourselves. So, Eris brings us sacred truth, but we have to be able to hear her message, and we have to ground it in reality by doing something about it. This is the secret to handling her heat: we have to embody her insight by acting on it, and then she becomes an endless source of sensitive strength.

## Eris Consciousness Challenges

We see in our research at the Dwarf Planet University, how, by simply making these new planets conscious, students become empowered, and their lives are transformed. To do this we need to engage with these new consciousness energies, and by engaging, we take them out of the unconscious arena of action.

To enable this engagement, here are some consciousness challenges for Eris. These are exercises to help us engage with this new aspect of consciousness, so we can on-board her energy in our lives. As we do, we will find ourselves becoming empowered and our lives will be transformed.

This section might be better titled, 'Dealing with Eris Consciousness Challenges' because she frequently manifests in our lives as challenges to our consciousness that we have to deal with. These exercises will be best focused in the area of your life represented by your Eris house position.

1. **Stop fooling yourself.** We often fool ourselves by what we say to others. To the question *"How are you?"* we say, *"I'm fine,"* rather than articulating what's really going on. Start self-correcting these self-fooling moments by being brave enough to be more authentic.

2. **Accept the opposing view.** If you're in a confrontation, examine what would need to change on either side to reach an accommodation. Is there a way to allow the opposing view so you can both live in harmony? If there is, make moves to enable that. If there isn't, quit the dispute.

3. **Practice compassion in action.** Reach out to someone in your world who is in need and lend a helping hand to enable their survival. This is a practical way to transmute life into love.

4. **Ground Eris practically.** Next time you can see something clearly in an Eris way, look for what small and immediate step you can take to manifest that vision. And then take that step and don't second guess it. That step leads to another, so take that and keep taking appropriate action to manifest your clarity. It is through acting that we ground her sacred wisdom.

5. **Reveal a hidden facet.** Search out a neglected side of yourself that you would like to develop and give yourself permission to find a way to do that. Then take the first step to do it. Tell yourself that, *"It's good if this is incongruous with my normal life, because it is enabling greater authenticity."*

6. **Know when to get off your high horse.** When you next find yourself rising to an Eris challenge, stay sensitive to when you have already won. There is a point at which continuing the battle turns it into a strategic defeat, by arousing more enmity than it allays. And when that moment comes, although there may still be stragglers on the battlefield, declare victory and de-escalate. This is hard to do, because the power is with you and there is still work to do, but you can transmute that into love and compassion by pulling your head in and leaving well enough alone.

## Case Study – Malala Yousafzai

Case studies enable us to see how Eris manifests in someone's life and thereby develop our understanding of the action of the planet.

Malala Yousafzai first came to world attention as a child campaigner for women's rights in Afghanistan. She has Eris closely conjunct Saturn, so she embodies the planet's truth-telling energy and feels a responsibility to speak out about her rights. We see this conjunction in her close relationship with her father, who she describes as her ally and inspiration.

> *Her father was a teacher and ran a girls' school in her village. She loved school. But everything changed when the Taliban took control of their town in the Swat Valley. The extremists banned many things and enforced harsh punishments for those who defied their orders. And they said girls could no longer go to school.*[4]

Her Eris is also closely square to her Sun in the 11th House of collective consciousness, so this challenged her to speak out publicly on behalf of girls and their right to learn. Her Eris-Saturn conjunction is in the 8th house of 'sensitivity to the deeper meaning' and in the interviews and meetings with government officials as a child, she spoke with a maturity about her right to education which was as if she was blessed with higher insight.

The 8th house is also the house of life and death, and her Eris-Saturn conjunction is sesquiquadrate her Pluto in her 4th house of emotional ground. This placement can bring power struggles affecting her emotional ground, and the sesquiquadrate says that these will challenge her Eris embodiment.

Her Pluto is conjunct Ixion, our new planet of seeker consciousness, which is conjunct her IC. Ixion is Pluto's lawless brother who is always pushing us to follow our passion, to be authentic, and if we step on any toes in that process, to ask for forgiveness afterwards rather than permission before. If we're not being authentic however, and childhood is frequently a time when we are trying to fit in, then we experience this energy in projected form as undesirable people coming into our life to push us to be ourselves.

4 https://malala.org/malalas-story

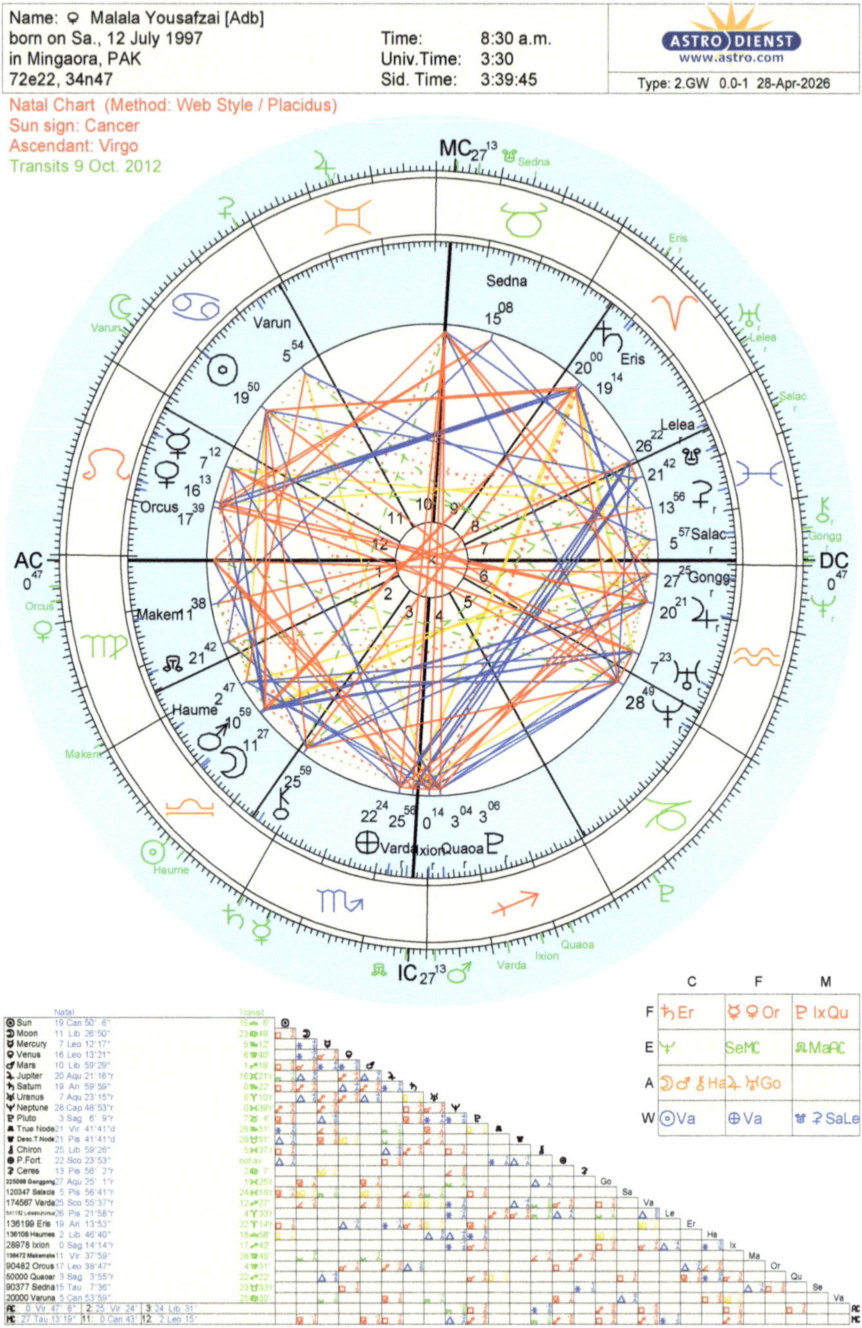

| Name: ♀ Malala Yousafzai [Adb] | | |
|---|---|---|
| born on Sa., 12 July 1997 | Time: 8:30 a.m. | |
| in Mingaora, PAK | Univ.Time: 3:30 | |
| 72e22, 34n47 | Sid. Time: 3:39:45 | Type: 2.GW 0.0-1 28-Apr-2026 |

Natal Chart (Method: Web Style / Placidus)
Sun sign: Cancer
Ascendant: Virgo
Transits 9 Oct. 2012

| | Natal | Transit |
|---|---|---|
| ☉ Sun | 19 Can 50' 6" | 16 ♎ 6' |
| ☽ Moon | 11 Lib 26'50" | 23 ♋ 49' |
| ☿ Mercury | 7 Leo 12'17" | 5 ♏ 12' |
| ♀ Venus | 16 Leo 13'21" | 6 ♍ 40' |
| ♂ Mars | 10 Lib 59'29" | 1 ♐ 19' |
| ♃ Jupiter | 20 Aqu 21'16"r | 16 ♊ 21'r |
| ♄ Saturn | 19 Ari 59'59" | 0 ♏ 22' |
| ♅ Uranus | 7 Aqu 23'15"r | 6 ♈ 10'r |
| ♆ Neptune | 28 Cap 48'53"r | 0 ♓ 39'r |
| ♇ Pluto | 3 Sag 6' 9"r | 7 ♑ 4' |
| ☊ True Node | 21 Vir 41'41"d | 26 ♏ 51' |
| ☋ Desc.T.Node | 21 Pis 41'41"d | 26 ♉ 51' |
| ⚷ Chiron | 25 Lib 59'26" | 5 ♓ 37'r |
| ⊕ P.Fort. | 22 Sco 23'53" | not av |
| ⚳ Ceres | 13 Pis 56' 2"r | 2 ♋ 7' |
| 225088 Gonggong | 27 Aqu 25' 1"r | 1 ♓ 25'r |
| 120347 Salacia | 5 Pis 56'41"r | 24 ♓ 18'r |
| 174567 Varda | 25 Sco 55'37"r | 12 ♐ 27' |
| 541132 Leleakuhonua | 26 Pis 21'58"r | 4 ♈ 33'r |
| 136199 Eris | 19 Ari 13'53" | 22 ♈ 14'r |
| 136108 Haumea | 2 Lib 46'40" | 18 ♎ 58' |
| 28978 Ixion | 0 Sag 14'14"r | 17 ♐ 42' |
| 136472 Makemake | 11 Vir 37'59" | 28 ♍ 46' |
| 90482 Orcus | 17 Leo 38'47" | 4 ♍ 31' |
| 50000 Quaoar | 3 Sag 3'55"r | 22 ♐ 22' |
| 90377 Sedna | 15 Tau 7'36" | 23 ♉ 33'r |
| 20000 Varuna | 5 Can 53'59" | 25 ♋ 30' |

| AC: 0 Vir 47' 8" | 2: 25 Vir 24' | 3: 24 Lib 31' |
|---|---|---|
| MC: 27 Tau 13'19" | 11: 0 Can 43' | 12: 2 Leo 15' |

| | C | F | M |
|---|---|---|---|
| F | ♄Er | ☿♀Or | ♇IxQu |
| E | ♆ | SeMC | ☊MaAC |
| A | ☽♂⚷Ha | ♃♅Go | |
| W | ☉Va | ⊕Va | ☋⚳SaLe |

## Shot by Taliban

Her outspokenness on her right to education made her a target for the Taliban and, when she was 15, on her way home from school, a masked gunman boarded her school bus, asked for her by name and shot her in the head. She woke up 10 days later in a hospital in Birmingham, England. She was shot because her truth that she did have the right to go to school was so strong that she was threatening the entrenched power system in the country.

The transiting planets show how we are developing the energies that they represent, and their aspects to natal Eris talk of that influence on our truth-telling inner guide. Transiting Eris meanwhile is talking about our developing truth-telling ability, our developing diversity consciousness.

She was shot on 9 October 2012, in the Swat District, Afghanistan. On that day, the transiting Sun was opposite her natal Eris within 3 degrees, and the transiting Moon was square within 4 degrees. These are wide aspects, but they do signify the importance of the event for her. And within one degree we have transiting Chiron semi-square Eris, speaking of the wounding danger that she was in and the healing that would follow.

However, one of the closest aspects, just 15 minutes from exact, is an opposition from transiting Haumea in the 2nd house. Haumea is our new planet of unity consciousness, who awakens us to the magic of being alive. She brings rebirth into our lives, and we have to gracefully surrender the old, or this rejuvenation can be experienced as tumultuous or violent. So, the Haumea opposition from the 2nd house represents a violent rebirth caused by events in the physical world.

Fortunately, there was also a close quintile from transiting Ceres, the inner dwarf planet of nurture, in the 11th house of collective consciousness. This grace thrust her into the collective consciousness as news of the attack spread worldwide, which enabled the prayers and financial support that spirited her from the bus in Afghanistan to a hospital in England and saved her life.

And this was assisted by a close sesquiquadrate from transiting Orcus, our new planet of karmic consciousness, in her first house of identity. Orcus gives us the stamina and reserves to deal with the crises in our lives. And at the top level he enables us to transmute shadow into light, in this case enabling Malala to transmute the shadow of the attack into a global consciousness raising event.

Eris moves very slowly and so Eris transits represent phases in our lives rather than specific events. However, the closer the orb, the more likely we will see the manifestation in the real world. When Malala was shot, Eris was closely inconjunct both her North Node in the 1st house and her Part of Fortune in the 3rd house. These aspects show the fateful nature of the attack for her personal destiny and for her ability to communicate.

Remember, in her natal chart she has Eris closely conjunct Saturn and closely square her Sun, and on the day of the shooting transiting Eris was still within 2 degrees of her Saturn and square her Sun within 2 degrees. Eris was also transiting in an approaching opposition to her Chiron within 3 degrees. These aspects show the existential challenge of the wounding event and the long period of healing that was going to be required as the opposition to Chiron perfected.

Finally, Eris is closely sextile her Jupiter in the 6$^{th}$ house of service in her natal chart, which is what brought her to public attention, speaking her truth at such a young age. And thankfully transiting Eris was still closely sextile her Jupiter when she was attacked, showing the expansion of her life which was to come from this point. The family relocated to England where she recovered, continued her human rights work and finished her education.

### Malala Fund

Her natal Eris-Saturn conjunction is closely trine her natal Venus in the 12$^{th}$ house of institutions and closely quintile her natal Uranus in the 6$^{th}$ house of service. She became a powerful human rights campaigner while still a teenager, then, together with her father, she established the Malala Fund when she was 16, which is a charity dedicated to giving every girl an opportunity to achieve a future she chooses.

> *Every day I fight to ensure all girls receive 12 years of free, safe, quality education. I travel to many countries to meet girls fighting poverty, wars, child marriage and gender discrimination to go to school. The Malala Fund is working so that their stories, like mine, can be heard around the world. We invest in developing country educators and activists, like my father, and we hold leaders accountable for their promises to girls.*[5]

5 https://malala.org/malalas-story

| Name: ♀ Malala Yousafzai [Adb] | | |
|---|---|---|
| born on Sa., 12 July 1997 | Time: | 8:30 a.m. |
| in Mingaora, PAK | Univ.Time: | 3:30 |
| 72e22, 34n47 | Sid. Time: | 3:39:45 |

Type: 2.GW 0.0-1 4-Mai-2026

Natal Chart (Method: Web Style / Placidus)
Sun sign: Cancer
Ascendant: Virgo
Transits 10 Oct. 2014

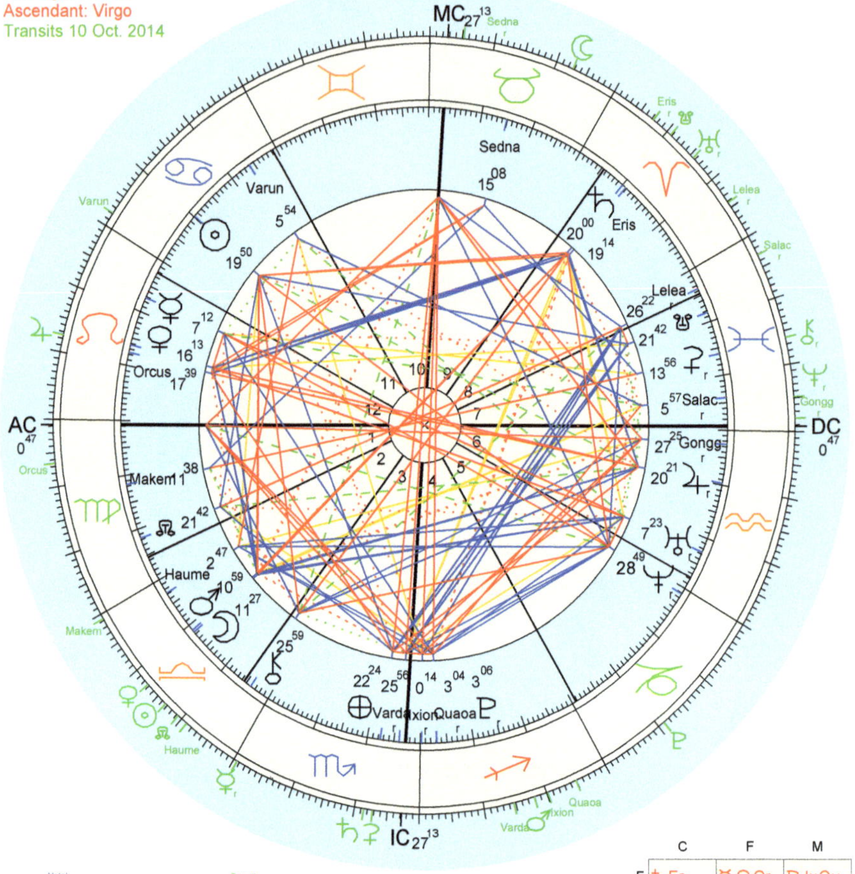

MC 27°13 · AC 0°47 · DC 0°47 · IC 27°13

| | Natal | Transit |
|---|---|---|
| ☉ Sun | 19 Can 50' 6" | 16♎37' |
| ☽ Moon | 11 Lib 26'50" | 7♉13' |
| ☿ Mercury | 7 Leo 12'17" | 0♏32'r |
| ♀ Venus | 16 Leo 13'21" | 12♎39' |
| ♂ Mars | 10 Lib 59'29" | 18♐ 3' |
| ♃ Jupiter | 20 Aqu 21'16"r | 17♌25' |
| ♄ Saturn | 19 Ari 59'59" | 21♏26' |
| ♅ Uranus | 7 Aqu 23'15"r | 14♈26'r |
| ♆ Neptune | 28 Cap 48'53"r | 5♓10'r |
| ♇ Pluto | 3 Sag 6' 9"r | 11♑ 4' |
| ☊ True Node | 21 Vir 41'41"d | 19♎14'd |
| ☋ Desc.T.Node | 21 Pis 41'41"d | 19♈14'd |
| ⚷ Chiron | 25 Lib 59'26" | 14♓ 0'r |
| ⊕ P.Fort. | 22 Sco 23'53" | not av. |
| ⚳ Ceres | 13 Pis 56' 2"r | 22♏47' |
| 225088 Gonggong | 27 Aqu 25' 1"r | 2♓ 2'r |
| 120347 Salacia | 5 Pis 56'41"r | 26♓56'r |
| 174567 Varda | 25 Sco 55'37"r | 14♐43' |
| 541132 Leleakuhonua | 26 Pis 21'58"r | 5♈51'r |
| 136199 Eris | 19 Ari 13'53" | 22♈41'r |
| 136108 Haumea | 2 Lib 46'40" | 20♎59' |
| 28978 Ixion | 0 Sag 14'14"r | 20♐12' |
| 136472 Makemake | 11 Vir 37'59" | 0♎45' |
| 90482 Orcus | 17 Leo 38'47" | 6♍31' |
| 50000 Quaoar | 3 Sag 3'55"r | 24♐57' |
| 90377 Sedna | 15 Tau 7'36" | 24♉46'r |
| 20000 Varuna | 5 Can 53'59" | 27♋54' |

| AC: 0 Vir 47' 8" | 2: 25 Vir 24' | 3: 24 Lib 31' |
|---|---|---|
| MC: 27 Tau 13'19" | 11: 0 Can 43' | 12: 2 Leo 15' |

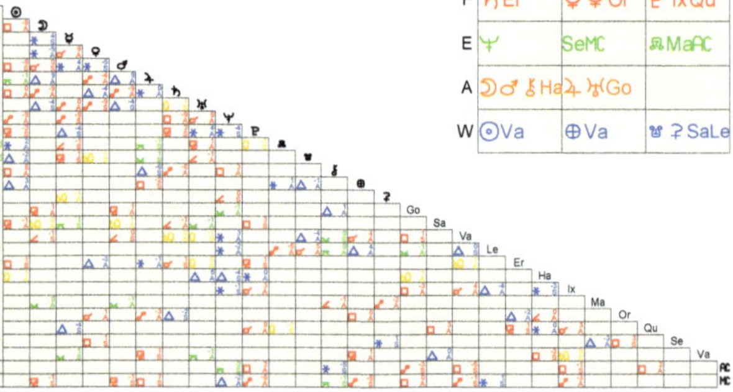

| | C | F | M |
|---|---|---|---|
| F | ♄ Er | ☿ ♀ Or | ♇ IxQu |
| E | ♆ | SeMC | ☊ MaAC |
| A | ☽ ♂ ⚷ Ha | ♃ ♅ Go | |
| W | ☉ Va | ⊕ Va | ☋ ⚳ SaLe |

Both her natal Eris and Saturn are closely biquintile her natal Varda, our new planet of inspiration consciousness, right at the end of her 3rd house, and conjunct the IC and Ixion. Varda is named after the Elven goddess from *The Lord of the Rings* who kindles the starlight, so she gives us the ability to shine our light in the world, or to find our way through times of darkness and despair, and to win the battles in our lives through hope and inspiration. The biquintile indicates an evolutionary flow where we can integrate the energies at either end at a deep level and bring it to a new synthesis. By surviving the attack and bravely continuing with her human rights work to enable girls to have a better education, she became an inspiration to many people.

**Receives Nobel Prize**

This work was recognized later that year when she was awarded the Nobel Peace Prize and became the youngest-ever Nobel laureate at 17. She was awarded the prize on the 10 October 2014 in Oslo, Norway.

That day the transiting North Node was closely opposite her natal Eris, with the South Node closely conjunct. This alignment with the transiting nodal axis shows the karmic nature of the experience, meaning that the award would enable her to resolve personal karma and to better fulfill her destiny.

Meanwhile transiting Mercury in the 2nd house of material resources was opposite her natal Eris as she received the award, which came with a cash prize of 4 million Swedish Kroner, about US$550k at the time. And transiting Jupiter in the 12th house was also trine her natal Eris, as her institution, the Malala Fund, expanded its activities and influence through her increased reputation and the influx of the new funds.

Just like when she was shot, the closest aspects from transiting Eris are an inconjunct to the North Node and an inconjunct to the Part of Fortune, showing again how winning the Nobel prize fatefully changed her destiny and enhanced her communication ability. We see here how these Eris inconjuncts can manifest in two completely different ways, which reaffirms that the outer planet transits are phases in our lives that must be interpreted from a bigger perspective rather than just one event. In each phase there is a development through a series of events, and, from that perspective, she had to be shot to win the prize. So, both inconjuncts brought a fated destiny resulting from her truth telling.

| | | |
|---|---|---|
| Name: ♀ Malala Yousafzai [Adb]<br>born on Sa., 12 July 1997<br>in Mingaora, PAK<br>72e22, 34n47 | Time: 8:30 a.m.<br>Univ.Time: 3:30<br>Sid. Time: 3:39:45 | ASTRODIENST www.astro.com<br>Type: 2.GW 0.0-1 28-Apr-2026 |

Natal Chart (Method: Web Style / Placidus)
Sun sign: Cancer
Ascendant: Virgo
Transits 22 June 2020

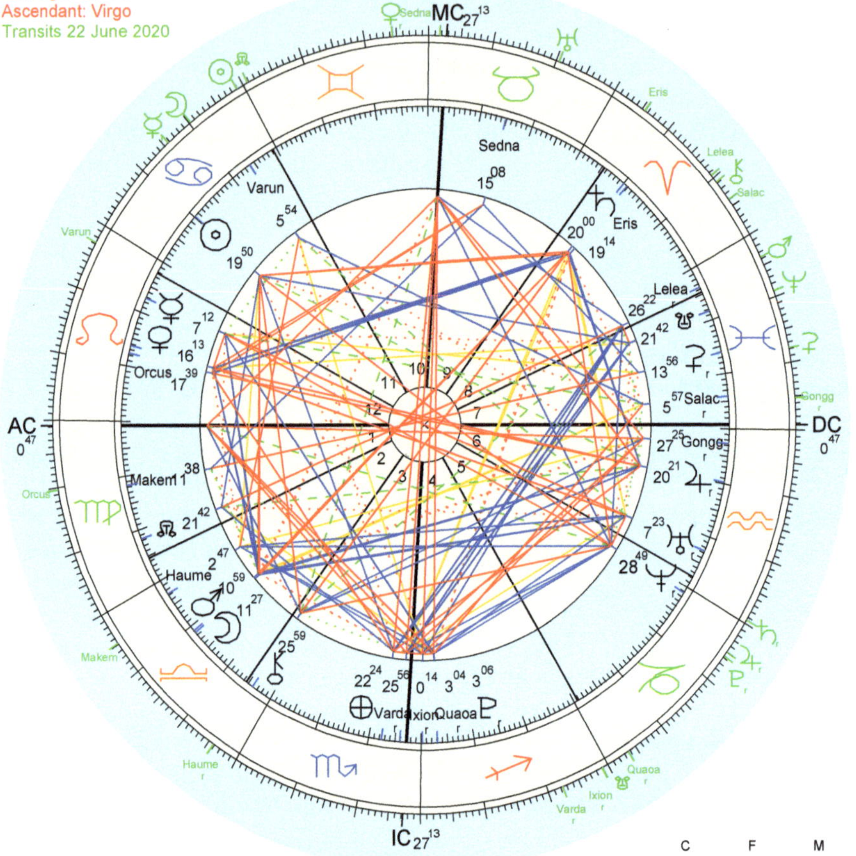

AC 0°47'
MC 27°13'
DC 0°47'
IC 27°13'

| | Natal | Transit |
|---|---|---|
| ☉ Sun | 19 Can 50' 6" | 1 ♋ 3' |
| ☽ Moon | 11 Lib 26'50" | 9 ♋ 45' |
| ☿ Mercury | 7 Leo 12'17" | 14 ♋ 14'r |
| ♀ Venus | 16 Leo 13'21" | 5 ♊ 33'r |
| ♂ Mars | 10 Lib 59'29" | 26 ♓ 16' |
| ♃ Jupiter | 20 Aqu 21'16"r | 25 ♑ 3'r |
| ♄ Saturn | 19 Ari 59'59" | 0 ♒ 38'r |
| ♅ Uranus | 7 Aqu 23'15"r | 9 ♉ 31' |
| ♆ Neptune | 28 Cap 48'53"r | 20 ♓ 58' |
| ♇ Pluto | 3 Sag 6' 9"r | 24 ♑ 18'r |
| ☊ True Node | 21 Vir 41'41"d | 29 ♊ 7' |
| ☋ Desc.T.Node | 21 Pis 41'41"d | 29 ♐ 7' |
| ⚷ Chiron | 25 Lib 59'26" | 9 ♈ 16' |
| ⊕ P.Fort. | 22 Sco 23'53" | not av. |
| ⚳ Ceres | 13 Pis 56' 2"r | 12 ♓ 10' |
| 225088 Gonggong | 27 Aqu 25' 1"r | 4 ♓ 46'r |
| 120347 Salacia | 5 Pis 56'41"r | 6 ♈ 4' |
| 174567 Varda | 25 Sco 55'37"r | 22 ♐ 24'r |
| 541132 Leleakuhonua | 26 Pis 21'58"r | 10 ♈ 32' |
| 136199 Eris | 19 Ari 13'53" | 24 ♈ 29' |
| 136108 Haumea | 2 Lib 46'40" | 25 ♎ 50'r |
| 28978 Ixion | 0 Sag 14'14"r | 29 ♐ 4'r |
| 136472 Makemake | 11 Vir 37'59" | 4 ♎ 51' |
| 90482 Orcus | 17 Leo 38'47" | 10 ♍ 18' |
| 50000 Quaoar | 3 Sag 3'55"r | 3 ♑ 45'r |
| 90377 Sedna | 15 Tau 7'36" | 28 ♉ 12' |
| 20000 Varuna | 5 Can 53'59" | 2 ♌ 45' |

| | | |
|---|---|---|
| AC: 0 Vir 47' 8" | 2: 25 Vir 24' | 3: 24 Lib 31' |
| MC: 27 Tau 13'19" | 11: 0 Can 43' | 12: 2 Leo 15' |

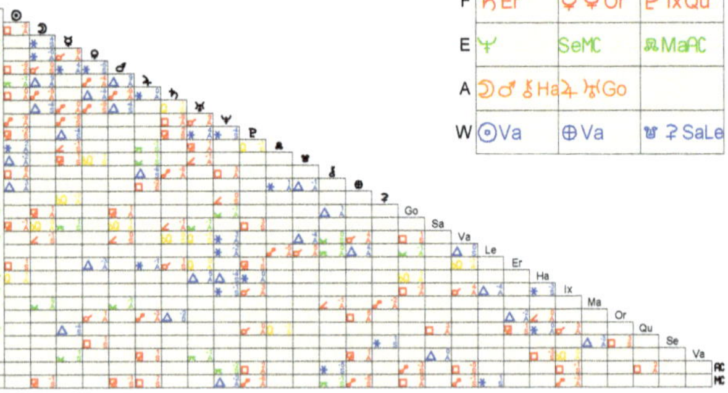

| | C | F | M |
|---|---|---|---|
| F | ♄ Er | ☿ ♀ Or | ♇ Ix Qu |
| E | ♆ | Se MC | ☊ Ma AC |
| A | ☽ ♂ ⚷ Ha | ♃ ♅ Go | |
| W | ☉ Va | ⊕ Va | ☋ ⚳ Sa Le |

## Graduates from Oxford

As you might imagine, for someone who was a child campaigner for girl's right to education, Malala really enjoyed studying for her Philosophy, Politics, and Economics degree at Oxford University.

> *I will always treasure my time at Lady Margaret Hall — the lectures, club meetings, balls and late nights (some spent finishing papers, some just chatting with friends in the dorm).*[6]

Let's have a look at the transits when she graduated. She announced on social media that she had completed her degree on June 22, 2020.

On that date transiting Eris, of course, was right on her 9th house cusp of higher education showing the karmic nature of the event. And it was biquintile her natal Ixion, our new planet of seeker consciousness, in the 4th house of home. We've seen the importance of her Ixion in encouraging her to be unapologetically herself and now on her graduation her developing diversity consciousness was in an evolutionary flow with her natal seeker consciousness.

Transiting Eris was also quintile Malala's natal Varuna, our new planet of mastery consciousness, in the 11th house of collective consciousness. Varuna is the higher octave of Saturn, lifting his permission-based authority into a natural sovereignty, but we have to claim this through action. Sovereignty is a dance that we do with the collective psyche, we have to claim it, and, at the same time, others have to agree to give it to us. So, the transiting quintile from Eris as she graduated is talking about the sovereignty in the collective consciousness that the degree was bringing her.

The Sun meanwhile was transiting in her 11th house, closely quintile her natal Eris, so her developing will was in an evolutionary flow with her inner spiritual guide. While Venus in the 10th house was semi-square her natal Eris, talking about the social recognition that the degree brought her.

This social connection was enriched by our new planet of empathy consciousness, Gonggong, in the 7th house of relationships, transiting semi-square her natal Eris. Gonggong is all about participating in the

6 https://malala.org/malalas-story

marketplace of life and finding the right place for us, or for our product, in that community interaction. So, the semi-square is talking about the enhanced position in the marketplace of life that the degree was challenging her to step into.

Malala has Gonggong natally in the 6th house opposite her Ascendent and in a T-square with her Ixion conjunct her IC. We saw earlier that this conjunction was one of the factors in her being shot, because Ixion can manifest as disreputable people pushing us to be ourselves. Gonggong at the unconscious level can also bring rage into our lives, so the natal T-square was key in the attack.

Now, however, as she graduates, Gonggong is transiting in her 7th house and is conjunct Salacia, our new planet of higher-love consciousness. We can look at Gonggong as the higher octave of Salacia, which we can see as the higher octave of Venus and Mars combined. Salacia lifts these inner planet's sexual connection into a psychic connection, and Gonggong steps that up into an ability to channel psychic, emotional and physical energy. So, the transiting semi-square between Gonggong and Eris as she graduated is challenging her to transition the joy and connection to community that she experienced in her student life into a deeper connection with the wider community through her human rights work.

## Case Study – Ian Channell: Wizard of New Zealand

Ian Channell is a British-born New Zealand eccentric who is the official 'Wizard of New Zealand'. He has Eris conjunct the ASC, so his truth telling ability is inherent in his behavior and his self-expression, and square his MC, challenging him to play the role of a diversity provocateur in society.

His eccentric philosophies are a mix of satire, playful contrarianism, rejection of dull conformity, celebration of magic and ceremony, and social commentary. He is less interested in dogmatically defending specific doctrines and more invested in making people think, laugh, and see the world from an unexpected angle.

So how did he become the Wizard? At 31 he graduated from the University of Leeds with a double honors degree in psychology and sociology. Then at 35 he joined the teaching staff of the newly opened School of Sociology at the University of New South Wales in Sydney, Australia. His Eris is sextile his Saturn conjunct Ceres in the 11$^{th}$ house, suggesting he will play a responsible and caring role in the collective consciousness.

His Eris is also closely opposite Varda, our new planet of inspiration consciousness, which is conjunct Ixion, our new planet of seeker consciousness, both of which are closely conjunct his Decendent. We saw in the previous case study that Varda gives us the ability to shine our light in the world, or to find our way through times of darkness and despair, and to win the battles in our lives through hope and inspiration. And that Ixion encourages us to be unapologetically ourselves and to follow our bliss.

During the student upheavals in Australia, which began at that time, he created a direct-action reform movement at the University of New South Wales, called 'Action for Love and Freedom' and he implemented this with what he announced to be 'The Fun Revolution'. The result was a revitalization of the university which was referred to in the Sydney Morning Herald as 'the university that swings'.

### Enters Radical Student Politics

So, let's look at Eris' action by transit in his chart at this time.

*"My involvement with radical university politics began in April 1968 at the University of New South Wales in Sydney."*[7]

In this period Eris was transiting in his 1st house closely trine his natal Sun Mercury conjunction on his 9th house cusp. So, his developing diversity consciousness was encouraging him to find his identity through communication in higher education. And it was also closely semi-sextile his North Node in the spiritual 12th house, and inconjunct his South Node in the service-oriented 6th house, so his developing diversity consciousness was pushing him to release karma in his daily routine and do his destined spiritual work.

Eris was also transiting semi-square his natal Chiron in the 2nd house, within 1 degree, talking about how his developing truth-telling ability would be motivated through this period by financial struggles. While at the same time Jupiter in the 6th house was transiting closely biquintile his natal Eris, offering an evolutionary opportunity to expand in his job and his daily routine.

In a condition of considerable financial hardship, he persuaded Melbourne University Union Activities Department to appoint him their unpaid 'Cosmologer, Living Work of Art and Shaman'. The vice chancellor gave him the use of a lecture theatre for his classes in 'synthetic cosmology' and the director of the National Gallery accepted the offer of his live body as a living work of art.

Transiting Chiron meanwhile was closely conjunct his natal Eris and his Ascendent, indicating a healing growth process was underway and suggesting a change in behavior as a result. Simultaneously, transiting Ixion and Ceres were conjunct in the sky in his 7th house, with both closely inconjunct his natal Eris. So, a maverick yet caring approach to his one-to-one relationships was fated to encourage this behavioral change.

He grew increasingly eccentric. He had long beard, and he blended magic, mysticism and sociology into a personal world view and began wearing robes and giving performances as a wizard. He called himself a "cosmologer," invented his own cosmology, and gave public lectures on the "Art of Wizardry", advocating for the magical transformation of the urban environment and turning mundane city life into something enchanted and spiritually vibrant.

7 My Life as a Miracle, The Wizard, Ian Channell, 1998

| | | |
|---|---|---|
| Name: ♂ Ian Channel [Adb] | | ASTRO DIENST www.astro.com |
| born on Su., 4 December 1932 | Time: 1:10 p.m. | |
| in London, ENG (UK) | Univ.Time: 13:10 | |
| 0w10, 51n30 | Sid. Time: 18:01:52 | Type: 2.GW 0.0-1 28-Apr-2026 |

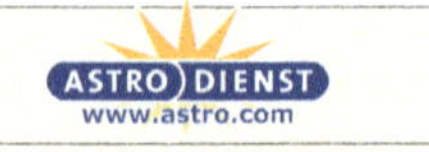

Natal Chart (Method: Web Style / Placidus)
Sun sign: Sagittarius
Ascendant: Aries
Transits 15 Apr. 1968

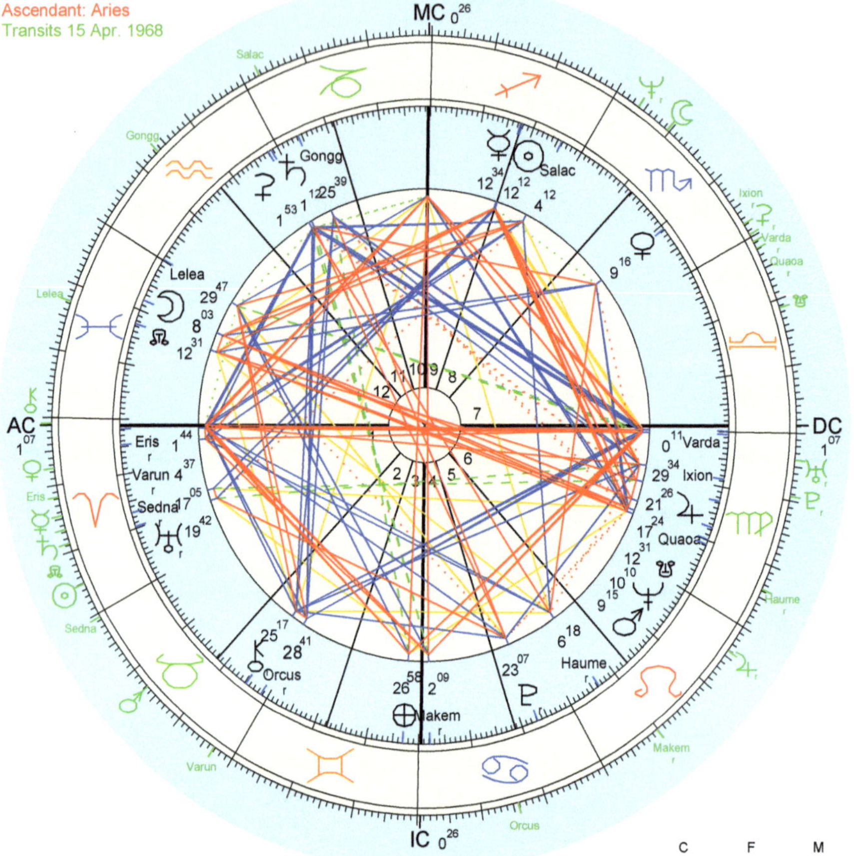


| | Natal | Transit |
|---|---|---|
| ☉ Sun | 12 Sag 12' 7" | 25♈ 5' |
| ☽ Moon | 8 Pis 2'34" | 20♏23' |
| ☿ Mercury | 12 Sag 33'47"r | 14♈31' |
| ♀ Venus | 9 Sco 15'43" | 7♈30' |
| ♂ Mars | 9 Vir 15' 5" | 13♉10' |
| ♃ Jupiter | 21 Vir 25'57" | 25♌54'r |
| ♄ Saturn | 1 Aqu 12'15" | 16♈36' |
| ♅ Uranus | 19 Ari 41'42"r | 26♍ 1'r |
| ♆ Neptune | 10 Vir 10'11" | 25♏57'r |
| ♇ Pluto | 23 Can 7'30"r | 20♍42'r |
| ☊ True Node | 12 Pis 31'29" | 18♈43' |
| ☋ Desc.T.Node | 12 Vir 31'29" | 18♎43' |
| ⚷ Chiron | 25 Tau 16'45"r | 0♈47' |
| ⊕ P.Fort. | 26 Gem 57'50" | not av. |
| ⚳ Ceres | 1 Aqu 53'29" | 0♏25'r |
| 225088 Gonggong | 25 Cap 38'56" | 16♒34' |
| 120347 Salacia | 4 Sag 12' 6" | 27♑17' |
| 174567 Varda | 0 Lib 10'31" | 29♎13'r |
| 541132 Leleakuhonua | 29 Aqu 47' 1" | 12♓34' |
| 136199 Eris | 1 Ari 44' 3"r | 11♈45' |
| 136108 Haumea | 6 Leo 17'59"r | 6♍17'r |
| 28978 Ixion | 29 Vir 33'49" | 2♏12'r |
| 136472 Makemake | 2 Can 9'21"r | 9♌57'r |
| 90482 Orcus | 28 Tau 40'39"r | 15♋53' |
| 50000 Quaoar | 17 Vir 23'33" | 28♎ 7'r |
| 90377 Sedna | 17 Ari 5' 7"r | 0♉33' |
| 20000 Varuna | 4 Ari 37' 8"r | 26♉48' |

| | | |
|---|---|---|
| AC: 1 Ari 7'23" | 2: 18 Tau 17' | 3: 12 Gem 17' |
| MC: 0 Cap 25'47" | 11: 18 Cap 40' | 12: 13 Aqu 1' |

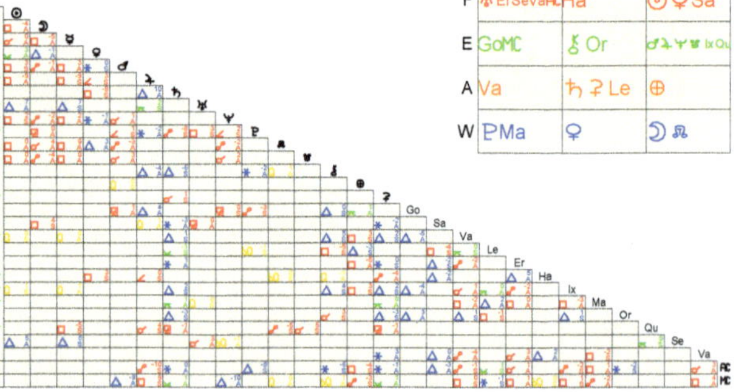


| | C | F | M |
|---|---|---|---|
| F | ♅ ErSeVaAC | Ha | ☉ ☿ Sa |
| E | GoMC | ⚷ Or | ♂ ♃ ♆ ☋ IxQu |
| A | Va | ♄ ⚳ Le | ⊕ |
| W | ♇ Ma | ♀ | ☽ ☊ |

This was also motivated by transiting Gonggong, our new planet of empathy consciousness, in his 11th house, which was semi-square his natal Eris. This transit was challenging him to connect with people on a deep emotional, psychic, and energetic level. Gonggong is all about participation and, at the top level, he's a spiritual wizard, able to raise the frequency of others from the inside and channel the energies we experience around us.

**Moves to New Zealand**

At forty-two, the Wizard moved to Christchurch in New Zealand and began to speak on a ladder in Cathedral Square. He often argued against widely accepted ideas simply to provoke thought, encourage independent thinking, and challenge social norms. He frequently critiqued government, bureaucracy, and "the system" for being overly controlling or obsessed with order and rationality. And he celebrated chaos, creativity, and unpredictability as necessary counterweights to bureaucracy.

He claimed that reality itself is shaped by human perception, ritual, and belief, saying: *"If you believe in magic and behave as if magic is real, then for you it is real".* He acted out magical rituals in public, suggesting that ceremony and spectacle can create meaning. And he encouraged people to not take themselves or the world too seriously, believing that laughter and absurdity are powerful tools against dogmatism and conformity.

Because his public speaking was not allowed under city council bylaws, the council attempted to have him arrested, but he became so popular that they made the square a public speaking area instead. So let's have a look at his transits when the Speakers Corner was designated on 17 February 1975.

On that day transiting Eris in his first house was still trine his natal Sun-Mercury conjunction on his 9th house cusp, within 1 degree, as it was more closely when he got involved in radical student politics. As in the previous case study, we see the phaslic nature of the slow-moving Eris transits, where the increasing eccentricity of his student politics set up his public speaking showdown with the council in Christchurch seven years later.

And transiting Eris was again closely semi-sextile his North Node in the 12th house, enabling him to do his destined work, and inconjunct his

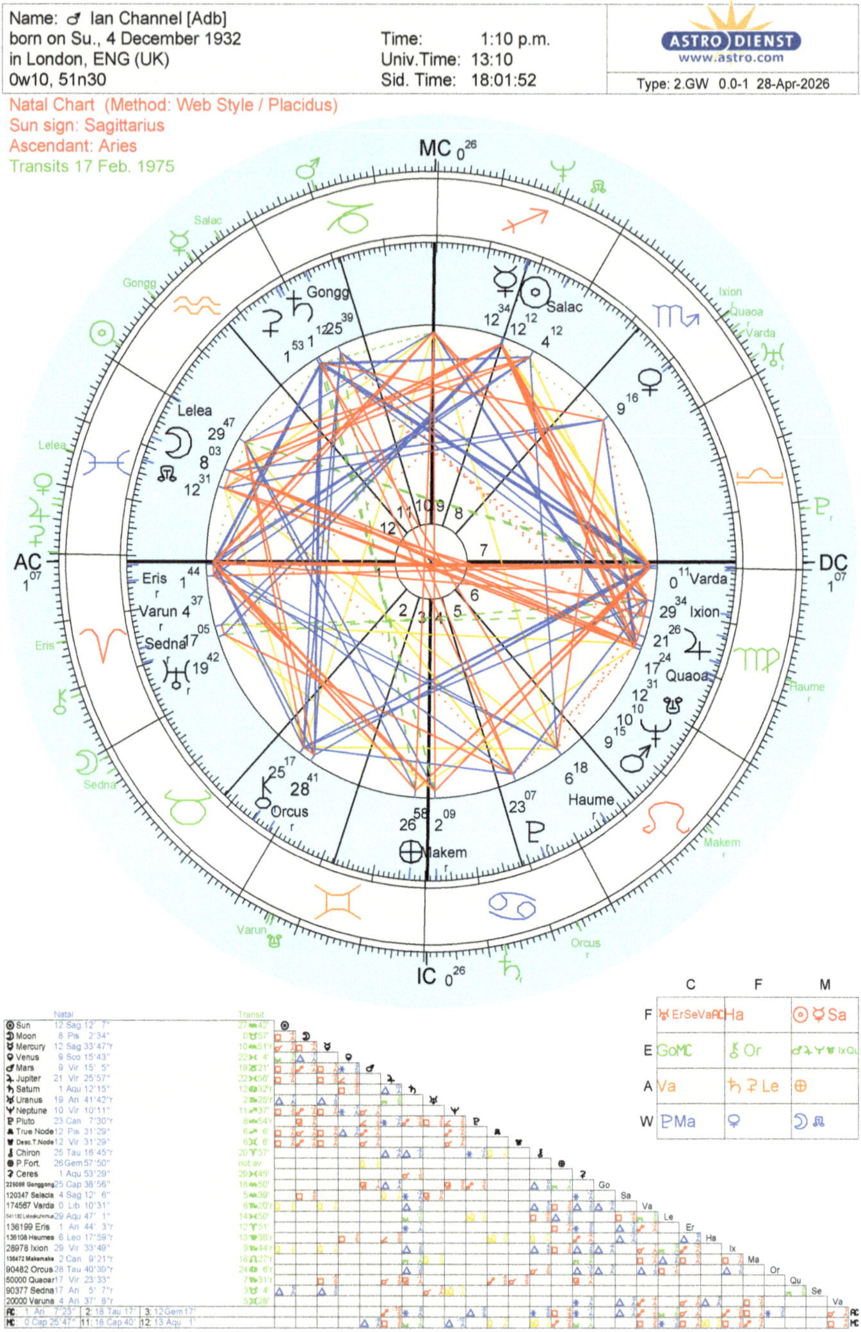

Name: ♂ Ian Channel [Adb]
born on Su., 4 December 1932
in London, ENG (UK)
0w10, 51n30

Time: 1:10 p.m.
Univ.Time: 13:10
Sid. Time: 18:01:52

Type: 2.GW 0.0-1 28-Apr-2026

Natal Chart (Method: Web Style / Placidus)
Sun sign: Sagittarius
Ascendant: Aries
Transits 17 Feb. 1975

| | Natal | Transit |
|---|---|---|
| ☉ Sun | 12 Sag 12' 7" | 27 ♒ 42' |
| ☽ Moon | 8 Pis 2'34" | 0 ♉ 57' |
| ☿ Mercury | 12 Sag 33'47"r | 10 ♒ 51'r |
| ♀ Venus | 9 Sco 15'43" | 22 ♓ 4' |
| ♂ Mars | 9 Vir 15' 5" | 19 ♑ 21' |
| ♃ Jupiter | 21 Vir 25'57" | 22 ♓ 56' |
| ♄ Saturn | 1 Aqu 12'15" | 12 ♋ 32'r |
| ♅ Uranus | 19 Ari 41'42"r | 2 ♏ 25'r |
| ♆ Neptune | 10 Vir 10'11" | 11 ♐ 37' |
| ♇ Pluto | 23 Can 7'30"r | 8 ♎ 54'r |
| ☊ True Node | 12 Pis 31'29" | 6 ♐ 6' |
| ☋ Desc.T.Node | 12 Vir 31'29" | 6 ♊ 6' |
| ⚷ Chiron | 25 Tau 16'45"r | 20 ♈ 57' |
| ⊕ P.Fort. | 26 Gem 57'50" | not av |
| ⚳ Ceres | 1 Aqu 53'29" | 29 ♓ 45' |
| 225088 Gonggong | 25 Cap 38'56" | 18 ♒ 50' |
| 120347 Salacia | 4 Sag 12' 6" | 5 ♒ 39' |
| 174567 Varda | 0 Lib 10'31" | 6 ♏ 20'r |
| 541132 Leleakuhonua | 29 Aqu 47' 1" | 14 ♓ 50' |
| 136199 Eris | 1 Ari 44' 3"r | 12 ♈ 51' |
| 136108 Haumea | 6 Leo 17'59"r | 13 ♍ 38'r |
| 28978 Ixion | 29 Vir 33'49" | 9 ♏ 44'r |
| 136472 Makemake | 2 Can 9'21"r | 18 ♌ 27'r |
| 90482 Orcus | 28 Tau 40'39"r | 24 ♋ 6'r |
| 50000 Quaoar | 17 Vir 23'33" | 7 ♏ 31'r |
| 90377 Sedna | 17 Ari 5' 7"r | 3 ♉ 4' |
| 20000 Varuna | 4 Ari 37' 8"r | 5 ♊ 28' |

| | | |
|---|---|---|
| AC: 1 Ari 7'23" | 2: 18 Tau 17' | 3: 12 Gem 17' |
| MC: 0 Cap 25'47" | 11: 18 Cap 40' | 12: 13 Aqu 1' |

| | C | F | M |
|---|---|---|---|
| F | ♅ ErSeVaAC | Ha | ☉ ☿ Sa |
| E | GoMC | ⚷ Or | ♂ ♃ ♆ ☋ IxQu |
| A | Va | ♄ ⚳ Le | ⊕ |
| W | ♇ Ma | ♀ | ☽ ☊ |

South Node in the 6th house, so his developing truth-telling ability was in a fated relationship with the karma which had brought him to this point.

However, transiting Eris was now also closely quintile his natal Saturn in the 11th house, which is an evolutionary flow between his public speaking and the rules and regulations in the collective consciousness, and this enabled a new structure for his participation in the city life. Wearing his costume as a false prophet of the Church of England or his wizard's pointy hat, he spoke in the square at lunchtimes in the summer months for over 40 years, entertaining the public with speeches, comedic acts, and eccentric philosophies and becoming a beloved local figure.

And finally transiting Eris was closely semi-square the Wizard's natal Orcus, our new planet of karmic consciousness, in the 2nd house of material reality. Orcus provides a code or a creed to live by and gives us the endurance and the tenacity to undertake the big tasks in our lives. By convincing the council of the benefit of his public speaking, a new code was put in place designating the square a public speaking area with no permit required. At the top-level Orcus enables us to transmute shadow into light and, by rising to the prosecution challenge, he turned it into an opportunity for everyone.

Meanwhile transiting Mars on his 11th house cusp was closely quintile his natal Eris, which was an evolutionary flow from the action he was taking in the collective consciousness, to the fearless self-expression of his Eris on the Ascendent. And transiting Uranus was closely inconjunct his natal Eris, so there was a fated push-pull between his networking ability and his self-expression as the prosecution threat was turned into the public speaking permission.

At the same time, transiting Quaoar, our new planet of spirit consciousness, in the 7th house was closely biquintile his natal Eris. Quaoar sings and dances the world into existence in myth, so this planet talks about a practice that brings spirit into matter. Yoga and meditation are well known practices that bring spirit into matter, but anything can be this sort of practice. Ian's performance as the Wizard was a practice that brought spirit into matter, and this was enabled at a deep level by the biquintile as the public speaking area was proclaimed.

**Appointed Official Wizard of New Zealand**

In 1982, when he was 50, the New Zealand Art Gallery Directors Association issued a statement that in their opinion the Wizard was an authentic living

| Name: ♂ Ian Channel [Adb]<br>born on Su., 4 December 1932<br>in London, ENG (UK)<br>0w10, 51n30 | Time: 1:10 p.m.<br>Univ.Time: 13:10<br>Sid. Time: 18:01:52 | <br>Type: 2.GW 0.0-1 28-Apr-2026 |
|---|---|---|



Natal Chart (Method: Web Style / Placidus)
Sun sign: Sagittarius
Ascendant: Aries
Transits 6 Oct. 1990

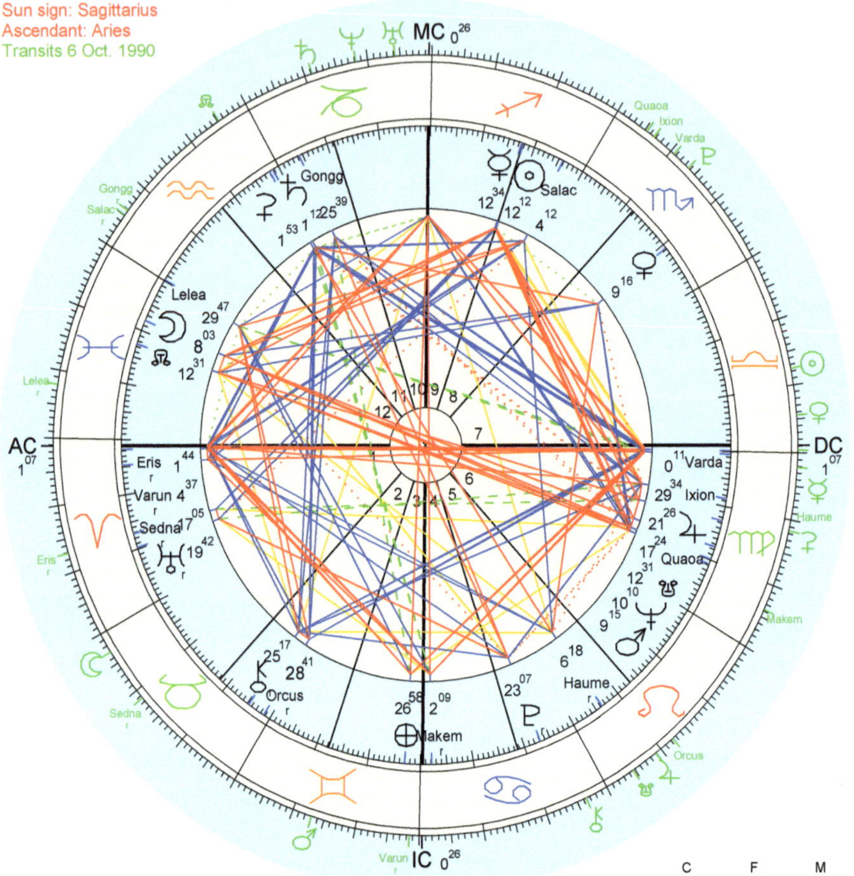

| | Natal | Transit |
|---|---|---|
| ☉ Sun | 12 Sag 12' 7" | 12 ♎ 29' |
| ☽ Moon | 8 Pis 2'34" | 3 ♉ 1' |
| ☿ Mercury | 12 Sag 33'47"r | 0 ♎ 27' |
| ♀ Venus | 9 Sco 15'43" | 5 ♎ 36' |
| ♂ Mars | 9 Vir 15' 5" | 13 ♊ 2' |
| ♃ Jupiter | 21 Vir 25'57" | 9 ♌ 5' |
| ♄ Saturn | 1 Aqu 12'15" | 18 ♑ 50' |
| ♅ Uranus | 19 Ari 41'42"r | 5 ♑ 48' |
| ♆ Neptune | 10 Vir 10'11" | 11 ♑ 50' |
| ♇ Pluto | 23 Can 7'30"r | 16 ♏ 21' |
| ☊ True Node | 12 Pis 31'29" | 4 ♒ 48' |
| ☋ Desc.T.Node | 12 Vir 31'29" | 4 ♌ 48' |
| ⚷ Chiron | 25 Tau 16'45"r | 26 ♋ 29' |
| ⊕ P.Fort. | 26 Gem 57'50" | not av. |
| ⚳ Ceres | 1 Aqu 53'29" | 18 ♍ 28' |
| 225088 Gonggong | 25 Cap 38'56" | 24 ♒ 7'r |
| 120347 Salacia | 4 Sag 12' 6" | 24 ♒ 55'r |
| 174567 Varda | 0 Lib 10'31" | 19 ♏ 21' |
| 541132 Leleakuhonua | 29 Aqu 47' 1" | 22 ♓ 1'r |
| 136199 Eris | 1 Ari 44' 3"r | 17 ♈ 5'r |
| 136108 Haumea | 6 Leo 17'59"r | 27 ♍ 52' |
| 28978 Ixion | 29 Vir 33'49" | 23 ♏ 16' |
| 136472 Makemake | 2 Can 9'21"r | 6 ♍ 15' |
| 90482 Orcus | 28 Tau 40'39"r | 12 ♌ 26' |
| 50000 Quaoar | 17 Vir 23'33" | 24 ♏ 39' |
| 90377 Sedna | 17 Ari 5' 7"r | 11 ♉ 21'r |
| 20000 Varuna | 4 Ari 37' 8"r | 26 ♊ 26'r |

| AC: 1 Ari 7'23" | 2: 18 Tau 17' | 3: 12 Gem 17' |
|---|---|---|
| MC: 0 Cap 25'47" | 11: 18 Cap 40' | 12: 13 Aqu 1' |

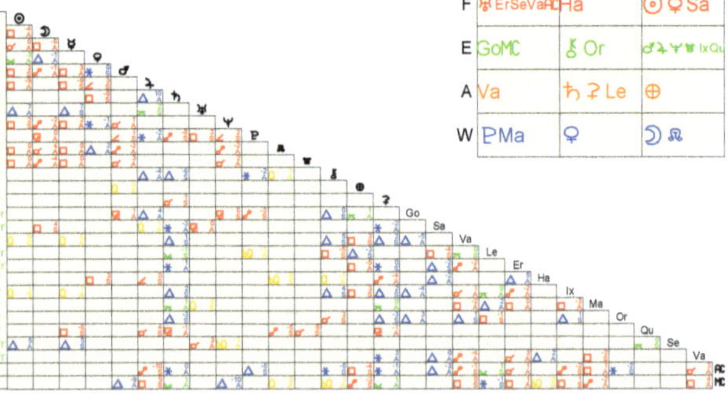

| | C | F | M |
|---|---|---|---|
| F | ♅ ErSeVaAC | Ha | ☉ ☿ Sa |
| E | GoMC | ⚷ Or | ♂ ♃ ♆ ☋ IxQu |
| A | Va | ♄ ⚳ Le | ⊕ |
| W | ♇ Ma | ♀ | ☽ ☊ |

work of art, and the Christchurch City Council appointed him Wizard of Christchurch. Then, on the 6th of October 1990, the Prime Minister of New Zealand appointed him the official Wizard of New Zealand.

In his letter announcing the appointment, the prime minister, Mike More, said: *"This appointment is made in recognition of the service you have given to the people of Christchurch and New Zealand and in the hope that you will continue to act as a Wizard and perform the traditional duties of a wizard. No doubt you will continue to enliven the spirit of the city with your wit, incantations, and philosophies. Your presence and wit have brought smiles to many."*

On that day, transiting Mars in the 3rd House was in a close quintile with his natal Eris, while transiting Saturn on the 11th house cusp was also closely quintile his Eris. So, both his developing action with ideas and communication, and his developing authority in the collective consciousness, were in evolutionary flows with his truth-telling ability.

Transiting Pluto in the 7th House was closely sesquiquadrate his natal Eris. So, the recognition of his public speaking was bringing about greater empowerment in his one-to-one relationships. Transiting Mercury on his 7th house cusp was opposite his natal Eris, within 1 degree, as the recognition of his truth-telling mission was communicated.

Meanwhile, transiting Eris was in a close conjunction with his natal Sedna, our new planet of soul consciousness, in his 1st house. Sedna talks about our spiritual destiny at the top level, but also about all of the work we have to do to get to that destiny. We can look at her as our *Soul's Path of Destiny* because her placement in our chart represents the growth experiences that our soul really wants to undertake in this life. The transiting conjunction from Eris, at the top-level, is all about fulfillment, so when we have done the work on our soul's path of destiny, the transiting Eris conjunction to natal Sedna is a time of spiritual fulfillment.

The spiritual fulfilment of the appointment was reinforced by Eris also transiting in a close biquintile with his natal Neptune in the 6th house of service. So, his developing truth-telling ability was in an evolutionary flow with the spiritual service he had been offering as the Wizard. He was appointed because his presence was seen to enliven public life and because his unique role helped promote Christchurch and New Zealand as quirky and open-minded.

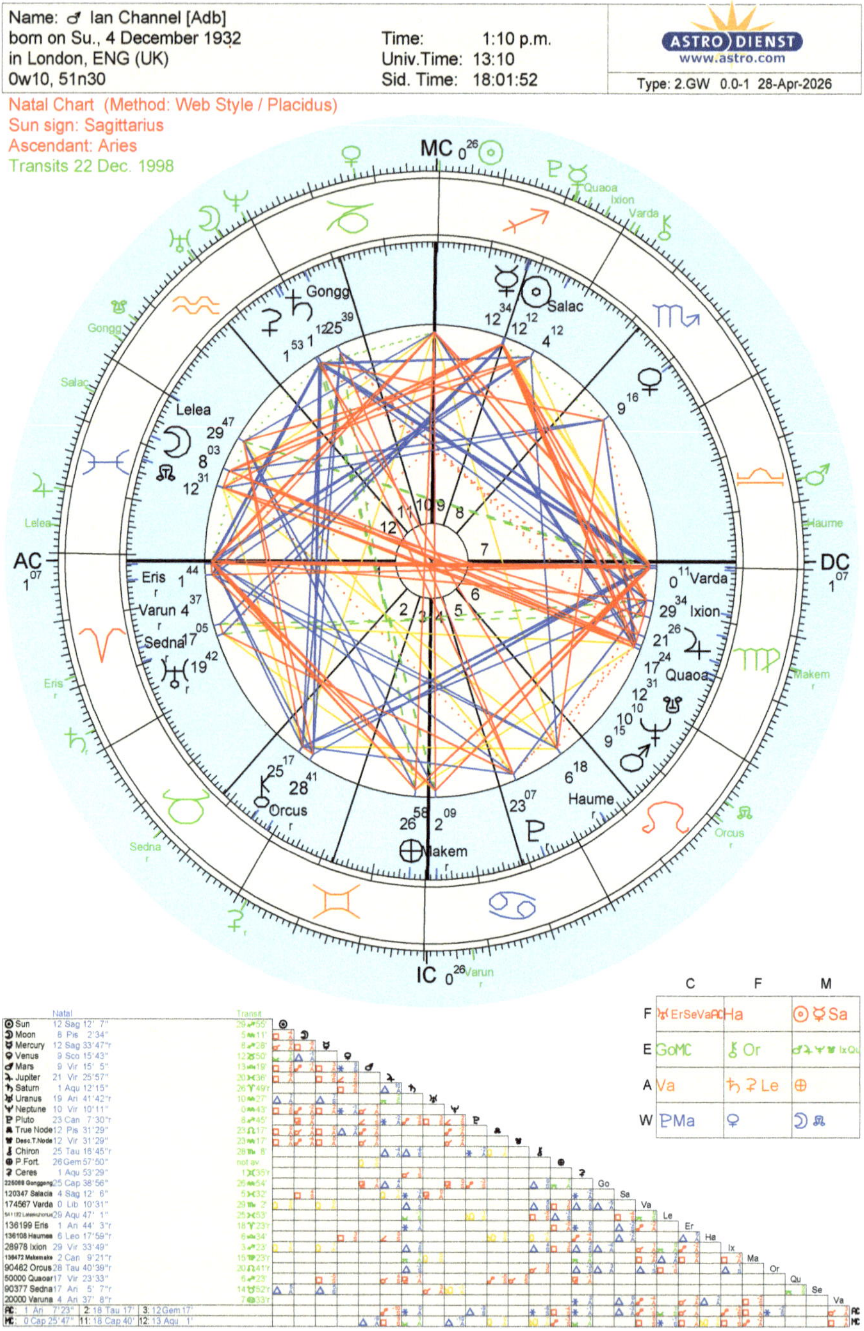

| | | |
|---|---|---|
| Name: ♂ Ian Channel [Adb]<br>born on Su., 4 December 1932<br>in London, ENG (UK)<br>0w10, 51n30 | Time: 1:10 p.m.<br>Univ.Time: 13:10<br>Sid. Time: 18:01:52 | <br>Type: 2.GW 0.0-1 28-Apr-2026 |

Natal Chart (Method: Web Style / Placidus)
Sun sign: Sagittarius
Ascendant: Aries
Transits 22 Dec. 1998

MC 0°26 · AC 1°07 · DC 1°07 · IC 0°26

| | Natal | Transit |
|---|---|---|
| ☉ Sun | 12 Sag 12' 7" | 29 ♐ 55' |
| ☽ Moon | 8 Pis 2'34" | 5 ♒ 11' |
| ☿ Mercury | 12 Sag 33'47"r | 8 ♐ 28' |
| ♀ Venus | 9 Sco 15'43" | 12 ♑ 50' |
| ♂ Mars | 9 Vir 15' 5" | 13 ♒ 19' |
| ♃ Jupiter | 21 Vir 25'57" | 20 ♓ 36' |
| ♄ Saturn | 1 Aqu 12'15" | 26 ♈ 49'r |
| ♅ Uranus | 19 Ari 41'42"r | 10 ♒ 27' |
| ♆ Neptune | 10 Vir 10'11" | 0 ♒ 43' |
| ♇ Pluto | 23 Can 7'30"r | 8 ♐ 45' |
| ☊ True Node | 12 Pis 31'29" | 23 ♌ 17' |
| ☋ Desc.T.Node | 12 Vir 31'29" | 23 ♒ 17' |
| ⚷ Chiron | 25 Tau 16'45"r | 28 ♏ 8' |
| ⊕ P.Fort. | 26 Gem 57'50" | not av. |
| ⚳ Ceres | 1 Aqu 53'29" | 1 ♓ 35'r |
| 225088 Gonggong | 25 Cap 38'56" | 26 ♒ 54' |
| 120347 Salacia | 4 Sag 12' 6" | 5 ♓ 32' |
| 174567 Varda | 0 Lib 10'31" | 29 ♏ 2' |
| 541132 Leleakuhonua | 29 Aqu 47' 1" | 25 ♓ 53' |
| 136199 Eris | 1 Ari 44' 3"r | 18 ♈ 23'r |
| 136108 Haumea | 6 Leo 17'59"r | 6 ♒ 34' |
| 28978 Ixion | 29 Vir 33'49" | 3 ♐ 23' |
| 136472 Makemake | 2 Can 9'21"r | 15 ♍ 23'r |
| 90482 Orcus | 28 Tau 40'39"r | 20 ♌ 41'r |
| 50000 Quaoar | 17 Vir 23'33" | 6 ♐ 23' |
| 90377 Sedna | 17 Ari 5' 7"r | 14 ♉ 52'r |
| 20000 Varuna | 4 Ari 37' 8"r | 7 ♋ 33'r |

| | | |
|---|---|---|
| AC: 1 Ari 7'23" | 2: 18 Tau 17' | 3: 12 Gem 17' |
| MC: 0 Cap 25'47" | 11: 18 Cap 40' | 12: 13 Aqu 1' |

| | C | F | M |
|---|---|---|---|
| F | ♅ ErSeVaAC | Ha | ☉ ☿ Sa |
| E | GoMC | ⚷ Or | ♂ ♃ ♆ ☋ IxQu |
| A | Va | ♄ ⚳ Le | ⊕ |
| W | ♇ Ma | ♀ | ☽ ☊ |

And finally, Eris was transiting inconjunct his natal Quaoar in the 6th house, which we've seen relates to his performance as the Wizard, bringing spirit into matter through that practice, which is why he became such a beloved figure. The inconjunct tells us that the appointment as the official Wizard of New Zealand was the fated result of the service that performance provided.

## Employed by the Council as Wizard

Following 16 years of providing the Wizard service pro bono after he was named as the official Wizard of Christchurch in 1982, he was finally signed to a contract by the City Council to provide "acts of wizardry and other wizard-like-services" on 22 Dec 1998. The contract, which initially paid approximately $16,000 NZD per year, lasted for 23 years until it was terminated in October 2021.

The closest transit with his natal Eris when the contract was signed was a sextile from transiting Ceres in the 2nd house of material resources. Ceres is our new inner dwarf planet, orbiting between Mars and Jupiter. She is actually a planetary embryo, the last one in our solar system, and she has an internal ocean. She talks about nurturing, and the give and take of love that keeps us alive. In the second house this love takes the form of income and, with the sextile to Eris on his Ascendent, it was income for his public speaking.

At the same time, transiting Ixion in the 8th house was trine his natal Eris, within 1 degree, talking about how his developing authenticity was bringing resources from the collective to assist his public speaking. And transiting Neptune in the 11th house of collective consciousness was sextile his natal Eris, also within 1 degree, talking about his developing collective consciousness vision that empowered his work.

*"The worst things in the world are stupidity, fear and hatred, and being serious,"* he told The New York Times in 1988. *"I want people to be enchanted and stop worrying."*

Meanwhile, transiting Eris was closely sesquiquadrate his natal Salacia, our new planet of higher-love consciousness in the 8th house of the resources that come from our one-to-one relationships. Salacia is appealing and she can bring a popularity, which in this case enabled and validated the social support. He was offered the contract because he was a beloved local figure.

Transiting Eris was also closely inconjunct his natal Quaoar in the 6th house of service, so the contract was the fated result of his ability to bring spirit into matter through his performance as the Wizard. It was also biquintile his natal South Node, which was conjunct his Quaoar and also in the 6th house, so his developing truth-telling ability was in an evolutionary flow with his karmic service.

When a transiting planet makes both an inconjunct and a biquintile to two planets in conjunction, the inconjunct is like a tease that enables the deep interconnection of the biquintile. So, the tease of his performance as the Wizard enabled him to live out his karmic destiny and be in the right place at the right time to sign the contract.

And finally transiting Eris was still conjunct his natal Sedna, our new planet of soul-growth, as it was eight years before when he was appointed Wizard of New Zealand. Eris is moving the slowest of all the planets at the moment and we can see the long phaslic nature of the transits she produces, where the spiritual fulfillment of the appointment as Wizard of NZ, developed over the following years, to enable public financial support. At the top level with Sedna, we learn to allow love and harmony and nurture abundance. When we face up to the soul-growth challenges in each moment we enable the abundance in our lives.

## Case Study – Alice Bailey

Finally, let's have a closer look at our higher-octave case study, Alice Bailey, who was an influential theosophical and esoteric writer whose works have deeply shaped the development of modern Western occult, New Age, and esoteric spiritual movements. Natally, she has Eris in the 8th house of the occult, and she taught that the primary purpose of human life is the evolution of consciousness, not just the perfection of our external circumstances.

She outlined a spiritual astrology in which planets and signs correspond to Rays, energies, and stages of soul development rather than purely physical destiny. As she saw it, spiritual development involves passing through successive stages called initiations, culminating in becoming a master. These initiations reflect an individual's increasing alignment with soul purpose. So, we can see that many of the ideas that are central to our modern spiritual thinking have come from the teachings of Alice Bailey.

As we saw in the higher octave case study, her Eris in the 8th house is quintile her close Pluto Haumea conjunction on the 11th house cusp and biquintile Mars on her ASC. Haumea is our new planet of unity consciousness, the higher octave of Neptune, who enables us to bring about a rebirth in our own lives and in the lives of people around us. On the 11th house cusp this rebirth occurred in the collective consciousness.

As she saw it, there are two great stages in the evolution of consciousness. First is the integrated personality stage where the focus is on developing strong, integrated personalities. In this stage the individual becomes capable, skillful, intelligent, and self-reliant, but is still often self-focused. Next is the soul-personality integration stage where true spiritual evolution begins and the personality comes under the conscious influence and direction of the soul. This involves transformation through discipleship, which she saw as a period of aspiring towards something greater, embracing service, and learning self-discipline.

Bailey's Eris is also square Venus in the 11th house of collective consciousness, so her higher guidance was challenging her to interact with groups that shared her values. We saw in the higher-octave case study that her Arcane School provided just such a group, and we'll see in a moment how joining the Theosophical Society was very influential in her spiritual development. Her teachings have also inspired numerous meditation groups, New Age organizations, influential astrologers, and esoteric healers worldwide.

In her chart, Eris is also sextile her Chiron conjunct Neptune in her 10th house, giving her a spiritual healing ability, which was strengthened by the Chiron-Neptune opposition to her 4th house conjunction of the Part of Fortune and Gonggong, our new planet of Empathy consciousness. Gonggong tunes us into the emotional, psychic and physical energies in the world around us and, at the spiritual level, he gives us an ability to channel those energies.

She thought of human beings as a system of physical, etheric, emotional, mental, and spiritual bodies, which all interact with subtle energies. She specialized in teachings on esoteric healing: using spiritual forces to help people heal and grow. She taught that true healing is found not just in fixing the personality, but by opening to the light and guidance of the soul, and that psychological crises and suffering are opportunities for "soul contact" and spiritual growth.

Her Eris is in a grand water trine with her Part of Fortune conjunct Gonggong in the 4th house of home, and with her Mercury in the 12th house of spirituality. We see the Part of Fortune in her being born into a wealthy middle class British family, and we see the Mercury in her Anglican Christian education and in all the books she published and the lectures she gave. While we see the Gonggong in her becoming a devoted missionary worker and Sunday school teacher, able to commune spiritually with groups of people.

### Her First Visitation

Let's look at how the occult guidance of her 8th house Eris manifested at some key points in her life. Her autobiography states that at the age 15, on June 30, 1895, she was visited by a stranger. *"... a tall man, dressed in European clothes and wearing a turban" who told her she needed to develop self-control to prepare for certain work he planned for her to do."*

On the day of the visitation the transiting North Node was closely conjunct her Eris in the 8th, as her destiny as a spiritual teacher was born. At the top level, Eris connects us with an inner wisdom or a higher wisdom, and we see how this manifested for Alice as a connection with a spirit guide. This connection was assisted by transiting Gonggong in

Alice A. Bailey 1932

| Name: ♀ Alice A. Bailey [Adb]<br>born on We., 16 June 1880<br>in Manchester, ENG (UK)<br>2w15, 53n30 | Time: 7:42 a.m.<br>Univ.Time: 7:42<br>Sid. Time: 1:12:49 | <br>Type: 2.GW 0.0-1 28-Apr-2026 |
|---|---|---|

Natal Chart (Method: Web Style / Placidus)
Sun sign: Gemini
Ascendant: Leo
Transits 30 June 1895

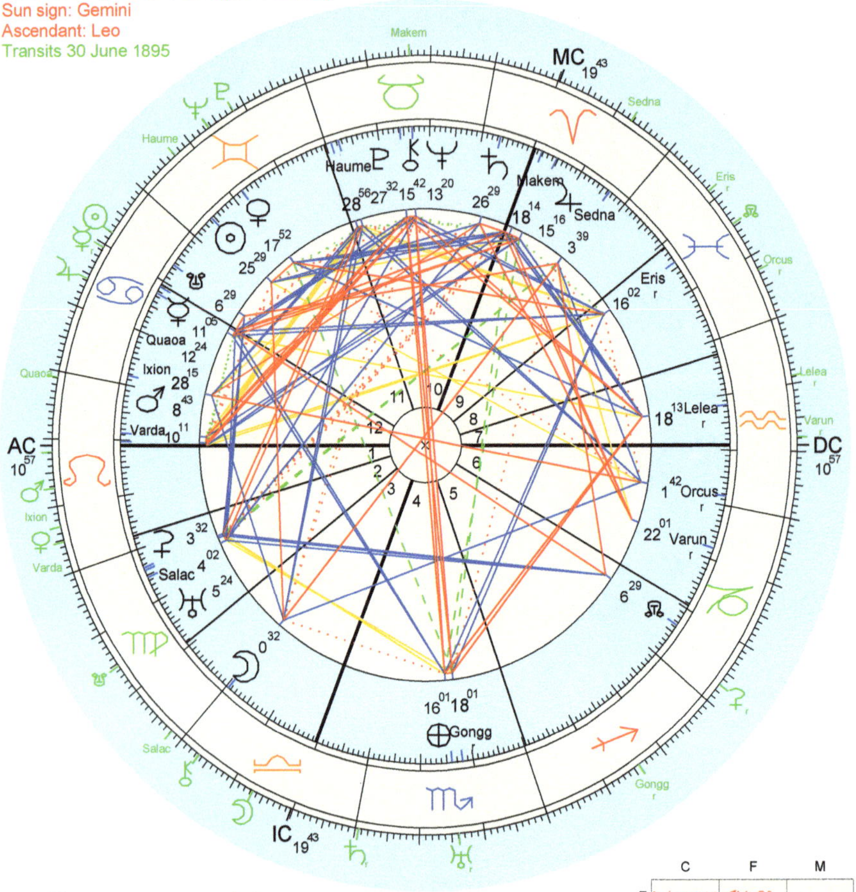

| | Natal | Transit |
|---|---|---|
| ☉ Sun | 25 Gem 28'33" | 7 ♋ 55' |
| ☽ Moon | 0 Lib 31'55" | 13 ♒ 18' |
| ☿ Mercury | 11 Can 5' 9" | 10 ♋ 25'r |
| ♀ Venus | 17 Gem 51'53" | 23 ♌ 0' |
| ♂ Mars | 8 Leo 43'22" | 11 ♌ 53' |
| ♃ Jupiter | 15 Ari 15'32" | 15 ♋ 36' |
| ♄ Saturn | 26 Ari 29' 5" | 0 ♏ 33'r |
| ♅ Uranus | 5 Vir 23'57" | 16 ♏ 7'r |
| ♆ Neptune | 13 Tau 20'29" | 18 ♊ 22' |
| ♇ Pluto | 27 Tau 32'12" | 11 ♊ 53' |
| ☊ True Node | 6 Cap 28'48" | 15 ♓ 24' |
| ☋ Desc.T.Node | 6 Can 28'48" | 15 ♍ 24' |
| ⚷ Chiron | 15 Tau 42' 2" | 3 ♒ 29' |
| ⊕ P.Fort. | 16 Sco 0'42" | not av. |
| ⚳ Ceres | 3 Vir 31'45" | 3 ♑ 2'r |
| 225088 Gonggong | 18 Sco 0'41"r | 15 ♐ 56'r |
| 120347 Salacia | 4 Vir 2'25" | 28 ♍ 5' |
| 174567 Varda | 10 Leo 11'22" | 25 ♌ 15' |
| 541132 Leleakuhonua | 18 Aqu 12'53"r | 21 ♒ 15'r |
| 136199 Eris | 16 Pis 1'59"r | 21 ♓ 29'r |
| 136108 Haumea | 28 Tau 56'11" | 22 ♊ 58' |
| 28978 Ixion | 28 Can 15'27" | 17 ♌ 16' |
| 136472 Makemake | 18 Ari 14'11" | 13 ♉ 17' |
| 90482 Orcus | 1 Aqu 41'42"r | 7 ♓ 38'r |
| 50000 Quaoar | 12 Can 23'43" | 0 ♌ 51' |
| 90377 Sedna | 3 Ari 38'55" | 7 ♈ 16' |
| 20000 Varuna | 22 Cap 1'23"r | 12 ♒ 13'r |

| AC: 10 Leo 57'20" | 2: 27 Leo 29' | 3: 19 Vir 15' |
|---|---|---|
| MC: 19 Ari 43'17" | 11: 0 Gem 20' | 12: 10 Can 39' |

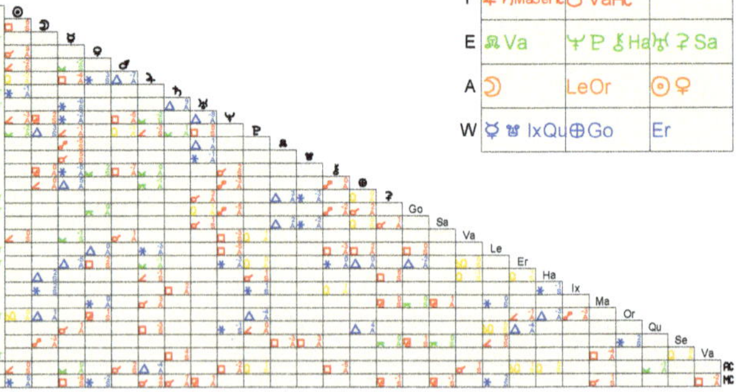

| | C | F | M |
|---|---|---|---|
| F | ♃ ♄ MaSeMC | ♂ VaAC | |
| E | ☋ Va | ♆ ♇ ⚷ Ha | ♅ ⚳ Sa |
| A | ☽ | LeOr | ☉ ♀ |
| W | ☿ ☋ IxQu | ⊕ Go | Er |

her 5th house, which was closely square her natal Eris, as her developing channelling ability enabled her to open to this guidance and embrace the higher truth that it embodied.

At the same time, transiting Jupiter in the 12th house of spirituality was closely trine her natal Eris, talking of the opportunity to do her spiritual work that this guidance would provide. Transiting Uranus, in the 4th house was also closely trine, tuning her into the psychic network and enabling the life changing connection.

Transiting Saturn in the 4th house was closely sesquiquadrate her natal Eris, challenging her to create a sacred space for the work she would do. And transiting Quaoar, our new planet of spirit consciousness, in her 12th house of spirituality, was also closely sesquiquadrate. Quaoar is a practice that brings spirit into matter, so her developing spiritual practice was challenged and strengthened as she embraced the Erisian occult guidance of the visitation.

Meanwhile transiting Eris in the 9th house was closely square the midpoint of her natal Sun Venus conjunction in the 11th house. So, her developing spiritual truth-telling mission was challenging her will and her values in the collective consciousness as she received the message that she had something to do.

And transiting Eris was also in a close sextile with her natal Varuna, our new planet of mastery consciousness, in the 6th house of service. We can look at Varuna as the higher octave of Saturn, lifting his permission-based authority into a natural spiritual sovereignty. And, as we've seen, sovereignty is a dance we do with the collective psyche, we have to claim it and at the same time others have to agree to give it to us. The challenge with Varuna is to claim this spiritual sovereignty, to stand forth and say, "I can do this", and the visitation gave her the spiritual permission to do this and to start her work.

Complimenting all this, transiting Neptune in the 11th house was closely square her natal Eris, talking of the spiritual challenge to the collective consciousness that her vision represented. She is credited with coining the phrase the New Age, which has shaped our modern view of spirituality, and the motivation for that work was this first visitation. She would go on to teach that humanity's evolution is guided by a plan administered by a Spiritual Hierarchy, aimed at leading the world into a new spiritual era, the Age of Aquarius, and that this age will emphasize group consciousness, world unity, and spiritual synthesis.

| Name: ♀ Alice A. Bailey [Adb] | | |
|---|---|---|
| born on We., 16 June 1880 | Time: 7:42 a.m. | |
| in Manchester, ENG (UK) | Univ.Time: 7:42 | |
| 2w15, 53n30 | Sid. Time: 1:12:49 | Type: 2.GW 0.0-1 28-Apr-2026 |

Natal Chart (Method: Web Style / Placidus)
Sun sign: Gemini
Ascendant: Leo
Transits 1 Sept. 1915

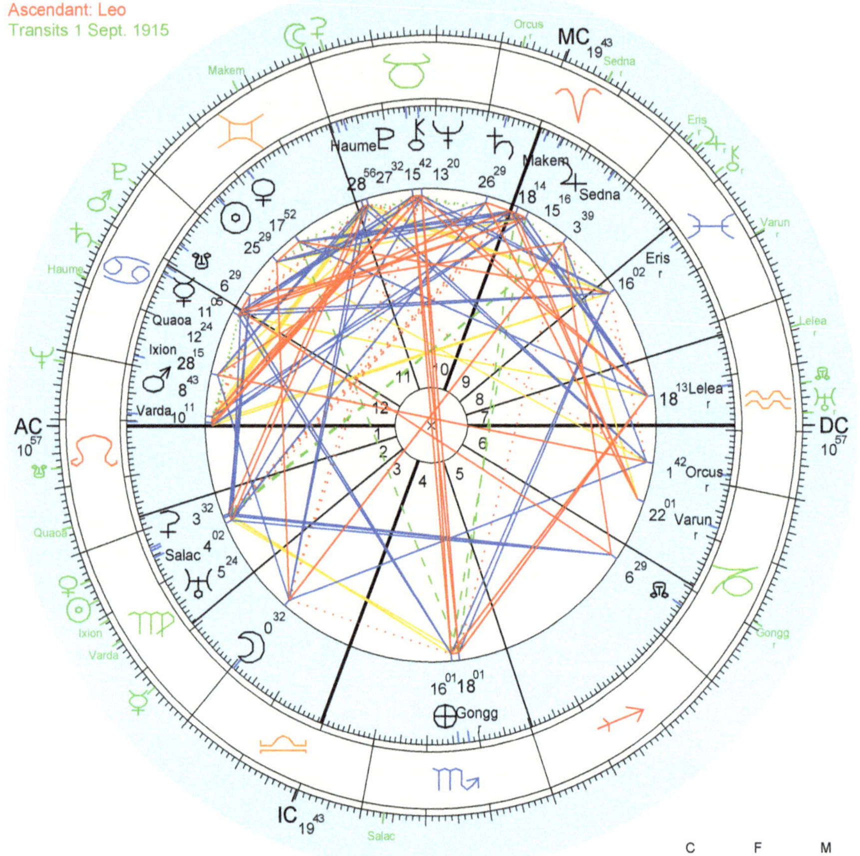

| | Natal | Transit |
|---|---|---|
| ☉ Sun | 25 Gem 28'33" | 7 ♍ 28' |
| ☽ Moon | 0 Lib 31'55" | 0 ♓ 41' |
| ☿ Mercury | 11 Can 5' 9" | 22 ♍ 58' |
| ♀ Venus | 17 Gem 51'53" | 4 ♍ 17' |
| ♂ Mars | 8 Leo 43'22" | 8 ♋ 5' |
| ♃ Jupiter | 15 Ari 15'32" | 25 ♓ 38'r |
| ♄ Saturn | 26 Ari 29' 5" | 13 ♋ 31' |
| ♅ Uranus | 5 Vir 23'57" | 12 ♒ 45'r |
| ♆ Neptune | 13 Tau 20'29" | 1 ♌ 32' |
| ♇ Pluto | 27 Tau 32'12" | 3 ♋ 7' |
| ☊ True Node | 6 Cap 28'48" | 17 ♒ 8' |
| ☋ Desc.T.Node | 6 Can 28'48" | 17 ♌ 8' |
| ⚷ Chiron | 15 Tau 42' 2" | 20 ♓ 58'r |
| ⊕ P.Fort. | 16 Sco 0'42" | not av |
| ⚳ Ceres | 3 Vir 31'45" | 27 ♉ 32' |
| 225088 Gonggong | 18 Sco 0'41"r | 10 ♑ 51'r |
| 120347 Salacia | 4 Vir 2'25" | 3 ♏ 32' |
| 174567 Varda | 10 Leo 11'22" | 14 ♍ 19' |
| 541132 Leleakuhonua | 18 Aqu 12'53"r | 25 ♒ 33'r |
| 136199 Eris | 16 Pis 1'59"r | 27 ♓ 34'r |
| 136108 Haumea | 28 Tau 56'11" | 18 ♋ 44' |
| 28978 Ixion | 28 Can 15'27" | 10 ♍ 44' |
| 136472 Makemake | 18 Ari 14'11" | 12 ♓ 1' |
| 90482 Orcus | 1 Aqu 41'42"r | 26 ♈ 36'r |
| 50000 Quaoar | 12 Can 23'43" | 25 ♌ 56' |
| 90377 Sedna | 3 Ari 38'55" | 12 ♈ 30'r |
| 20000 Varuna | 22 Cap 1'23"r | 10 ♓ 13'r |

| AC: 10 Leo 57'20" | 2: 27 Leo 29' | 3: 19 Vir 15' |
|---|---|---|
| MC: 19 Ari 43'17" | 11: 0 Gem 20' | 12: 10 Can 39' |

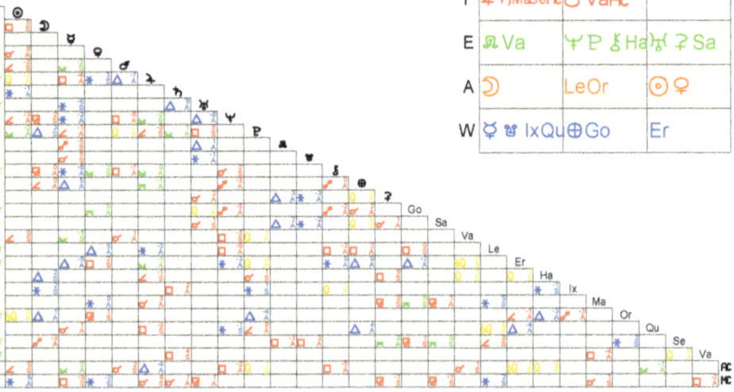

| | C | F | M |
|---|---|---|---|
| F | ♃ ♄ Ma Se MC | ♂ Va AC | |
| E | ☊ Va | ♆ ♇ ⚷ Ha | ♅ ⚳ Sa |
| A | ☽ | Le Or | ☉ ♀ |
| W | ☿ ☋ Ix Qu | ⊕ Go | Er |

## Joins Theosophical Society

Early on she was still searching for her path, however, growing out of the Anglican upbringing and her work as a missionary worker and Sunday School teacher. Then in 1915, when she was 35 and working in a sardine cannery in California in order to support her daughters, several women introduced her to Helena Blavatsky and Theosophy, and she began to study *Blavatsky's Secret Doctrines.*

Her later teachings, sometimes referred to as the "Ageless Wisdom Teachings," would build on this earlier work of Blavatsky, but introduce significant new material, so the Theosophical Society answered her natal Eris sextile Venus-in-the-11th need for a likeminded group to help develop her occult guidance. As Alice Anne Evans she was admitted as a member on September 1, 1915.

On this date transiting Neptune, now in her 12th house, was closely sesquiquadrate her natal Eris, so her developing spiritual consciousness was challenging her to take a new step in the development of her higher wisdom. Meanwhile, Eris was also transiting closely semi-square her natal Neptune and sextile her Pluto, both in the 10th, so joining the society was the answer to a challenge from her developing occult mission to find a spiritual place in society where she could bring about change.

Transiting Ceres was in the 10th house, closely quintile her natal Eris in the 8th house, showing how the Theosophical Society would provide a nurturing social environment for her occult Eris mission. And the transiting North Node in the 7th house was semi-sextile her Eris, within 1 degree, so her developing destiny in her one-to-one relationships was encouraging the move.

Transiting Saturn and Haumea, both in the 12th, were trine her natal Eris, within 2 degrees, talking about the birth of a new form of spiritual practice that was to come out of her joining the Society. These trines to her natal Eris were mirrored by a transiting Eris semi-sextile to her natal Saturn, and a sextile to her natal Haumea, both within 1 degree, emphasizing the structural and rejuvenating influence the Society would have on her life.

Finally transiting Eris was also trine her natal Ixion, our new planet of seeker consciousness, in the 12th house of spirituality. Ixion enables us

| | | |
|---|---|---|
| Name: ♀ Alice A. Bailey [Adb]<br>born on We., 16 June 1880<br>in Manchester, ENG (UK)<br>2w15, 53n30 | Time: 7:42 a.m.<br>Univ.Time: 7:42<br>Sid. Time: 1:12:49 | <br>Type: 2.GW 0.0-1 28-Apr-2026 |

Natal Chart (Method: Web Style / Placidus)
Sun sign: Gemini
Ascendant: Leo
Transits 15 Nov. 1919

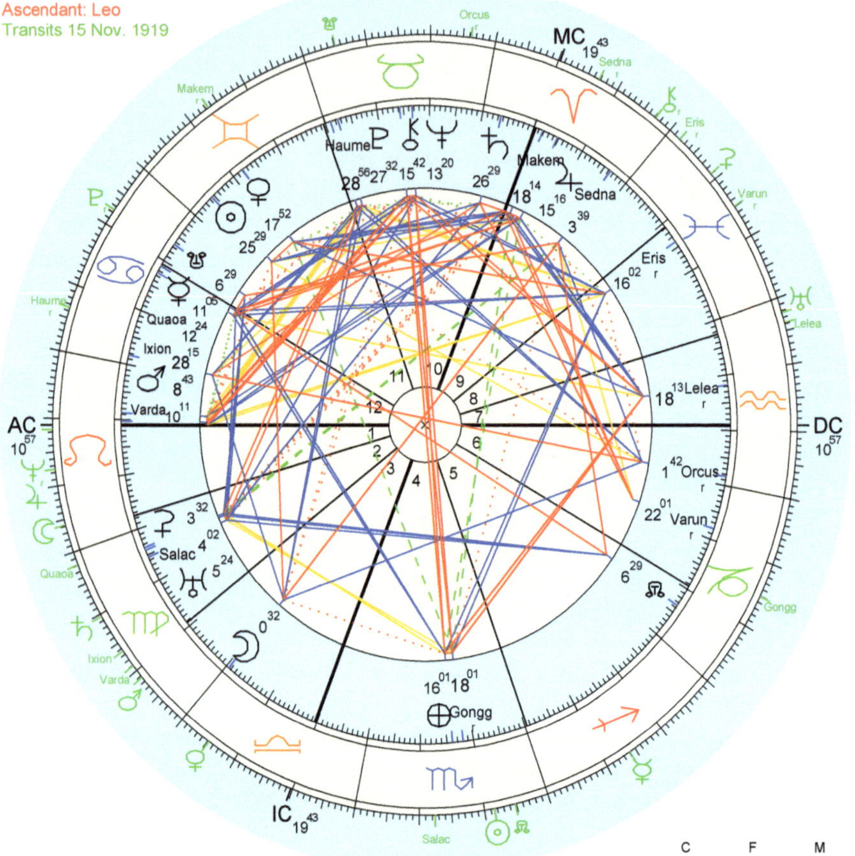

| | Natal | Transit |
|---|---|---|
| ☉ Sun | 25 Gem 28'33" | 21 ♏ 34' |
| ☽ Moon | 0 Lib 31'55" | 25 ♌ 49' |
| ☿ Mercury | 11 Can 5' 9" | 14 ♐ 6' |
| ♀ Venus | 17 Gem 51'53" | 5 ♎ 9' |
| ♂ Mars | 8 Leo 43'22" | 21 ♍ 15' |
| ♃ Jupiter | 15 Ari 15'32" | 17 ♌ 28' |
| ♄ Saturn | 26 Ari 29' 5" | 10 ♍ 22' |
| ♅ Uranus | 5 Vir 23'57" | 27 ♒ 48' |
| ♆ Neptune | 13 Tau 20'29" | 11 ♌ 33'r |
| ♇ Pluto | 27 Tau 32'12" | 7 ♋ 32'r |
| ☊ True Node | 6 Cap 28'48" | 24 ♏ 51' |
| ☋ Desc.T.Node | 6 Can 28'48" | 24 ♉ 51' |
| ⚷ Chiron | 15 Tau 42' 2" | 2 ♈ 53'r |
| ⊕ P.Fort. | 16 Sco 0'42" | not av |
| ⚳ Ceres | 3 Vir 31'45" | 21 ♓ 5' |
| 225088 Gonggong | 18 Sco 0'41"r | 14 ♑ 56' |
| 120347 Salacia | 4 Vir 2'25" | 12 ♏ 26' |
| 174567 Varda | 10 Leo 11'22" | 19 ♍ 4' |
| 541132 Leleakuhonua | 18 Aqu 12'53"r | 26 ♒ 15' |
| 136199 Eris | 16 Pis 1'59"r | 28 ♓ 2'r |
| 136108 Haumea | 28 Tau 56'11" | 23 ♋ 24'r |
| 28978 Ixion | 28 Can 15'27" | 16 ♍ 22' |
| 136472 Makemake | 18 Ari 14'11" | 16 ♊ 33'r |
| 90482 Orcus | 1 Aqu 41'42"r | 3 ♉ 46'r |
| 50000 Quaoar | 12 Can 23'43" | 1 ♍ 56' |
| 90377 Sedna | 3 Ari 38'55" | 13 ♈ 10'r |
| 20000 Varuna | 22 Cap 1'23"r | 15 ♓ 2'r |

| AC: 10 Leo 57'20" | 2: 27 Leo 29' | 3: 19 Vir 15' |
|---|---|---|
| MC: 19 Ari 43'17" | 11: 0 Gem 20' | 12: 10 Can 39' |

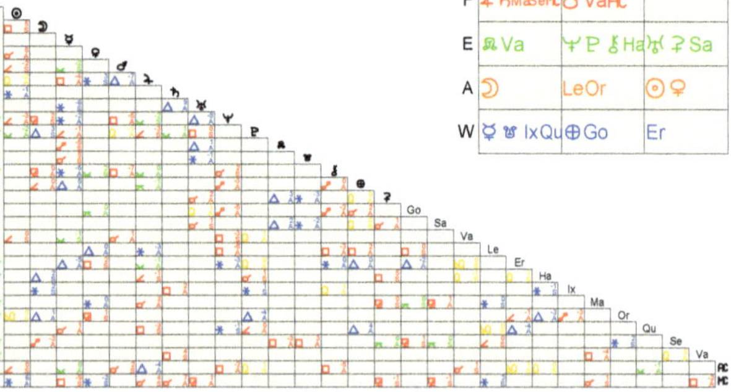

| | C | F | M |
|---|---|---|---|
| F | ♃ ♄ Ma Se MC | ♂ Va AC | |
| E | ☊ Va | ♆ ♇ ⚷ Ha | ♅ ⚳ Sa |
| A | ☽ | Le Or | ☉ ♀ |
| W | ☿ ☋ Ix Qu | ⊕ Go | Er |

to be ourselves and follow our spiritual bliss, so joining the Theosophical Society encouraged her authenticity and enabled her to find her unique independent approach to spirituality. Her membership continued, with short lapses, for the next 24 years.

### Tibetan Master Djwhal Khul appears

We've seen how her Eris in the 8th house trine Gonggong in her 4th house enabled her to channel spirit energies in her first visitation and, three years after she joined the Society, her "teacher" appeared, identifying himself as Tibetan Master Djwhal Khul. She wrote in her books that much of the material was telepathically transmitted by "The Tibetan", who she described as one of the enlightened Masters of the Spiritual Hierarchy. Channelling his guidance, she wrote a series of "ageless wisdom books on the teachings from Djwhal Khul" that became lauded as classics in occult teaching.

> *It was in November 1919 that I made my first contact with the Tibetan.*[8]

Interestingly, transiting Ixion, our new planet of seeker consciousness, in the 2nd house of material reality, was closely opposite her natal Eris as her guide manifested, giving a unique independent form to her higher wisdom. We've seen how the transiting Eris trine her natal Ixion as she joined the Theosophical Society was a key to enabling her seeker consciousness, and now with the transiting Ixion opposition to her natal Eris her seeker consciousness found a guide.

Gonggong, our new planet that at the top level gives us a channelling ability, was transiting in the 6th house of service, closely sextile her natal Eris, as she started channelling her spirit guide. This aspect was within 1 degree and it was approaching, which tells us that this connection would develop over the following years.

Signaling the fated opportunity that the manifestation represented, transiting Jupiter in the 1st house was inconjunct her natal Eris, while transiting Mercury in the 5th house was square, both within 1 degree. Together these suggest that there will be a fated growth in her identity if she can rise to the challenge of centering her communication in love. We can see that she did rise to this challenge because in her unfinished autobiography, she expressed her love and compassion for her teachers.

---

8 Bailey, Alice A. *The Unfinished Autobiography.* Lucis Publishing, 1951, p156.

Transiting Makemake, our new planet of systems consciousness, in the 11th house of collective consciousness, was closely square her natal Eris. Makemake is our model of the world and of our place in that world. A new-born baby sees colors and hears sounds but has no functioning Makemake to make sense out of these sensations. As her guide manifested, this square is talking about the richer understanding of the world that he would bring as well as giving her a way to work within that understanding to enable a growth in consciousness.

Bailey wrote extensively on the importance of occult meditation, of structured, purposeful exercises to align with the soul, contact spiritual energies, and serve humanity. She saw meditation as a tool to align the personality with the soul. And she saw service, doing selfless work, as a sure sign of soul contact and spiritual progress. She taught that the study of life's lessons was a key method of learning detachment, mindfulness, and discrimination.

And, finally, transiting Varuna, our new planet of mastery consciousness, in the 8th house of the occult was conjunct her natal Eris within 1 degree, as her enlightened Master manifested. This conjunction strengthened in the following years as it perfected, and it represents the start of a new cycle of her developing sovereignty in occult truth-telling.

Meanwhile the Eris transits are the same as 3 years earlier when she joined the society, again showing the phaslic nature of the outer planet transits. Eris was transiting square her Sun and opposite her Moon, both within 2 degrees. And the transiting Eris semi-square to Neptune and sextile to Pluto, both in the 10th, are still very close, as is the trine to Ixion. These aspects talk of the channeling she was doing and the unique form of the spiritual guide. The difference with the chart of joining the Theosophical Society is that the transiting Eris sextile to Haumea on the 11th house cusp has moved to be exact, so the rebirth that was foretold as she joined the Society, was actualized with the manifestation of her guide.

## Eris in the Signs

Eris is in the phase of her orbit where she spends a longer time in each sign and she's been in Aries since 1926, so virtually everyone alive today has Eris in Aries. This means that our whole understanding of Eris comes from an Aries perspective and this sign is ruled by her brother Mars, so this sojourn has encouraged the warlike understanding that we have of this new planet.

We are in a period of major, disruptive shifts in society, and Eris gives us the ability to navigate this chaos and deal with this environmental turbulence, while the Aries placement brings a spontaneous and fearless approach to this.

Many of us today are quick to speak out about the truth as we see it, happily provoking discord because doing so encourages the disruption of false harmony. Eris in Aries wants to puncture the illusions, reveal the secrets, and expose any hypocrisy we discover. We might also feel a righteous anger when we, or someone else, is treated unfairly or marginalized in some way. This is certainly motivating many of us to fight for our rights as we see it, or for human rights, and for equality, or to demand recognition in some way.

The danger is that we might be too impulsive with this outspokenness, failing to read how open others will be to our words, or to understand the consequences that our outburst might have. We could also be coming from a selfish perspective in this communication and feel a righteousness about out truth which doesn't consider the other perspective at all.

Aries can bring an impatience and a quick-tempered approach, and Eris can encourage us to go against the crowd or the norm, to act independently, often as a lone wolf. So, at the unconscious level we might feel slighted, marginalized, or forgotten by society in some way, and so might develop a "Black Sheep" syndrome and feel like an outcast or outsider.

The naturally competitive spirit of Eris is heightened by the similarly competitive nature of Aries, so, at the unconscious level, Eris is encouraging us to join the rat-race, because everyone else is. This can give us a malicious envy of others at the lower level, but it breeds a noble rivalry at the top level, which drives us toward excellence.

Eris in Aries is promoting our consciousness growth by encouraging us to leap into the competitive social system, and one way this can manifest is by leading us to an early or a sudden peak, to a success that 'comes too early', and which brings us to an eventual existential crisis later on, where we learn to see ourselves in a more spiritually wholistic way.

With this placement we have a mental sharpness which can give us the ability to see through deception and use deep psychological knowledge to understand a situation. It gives us the courage of our convictions and as a result we could become a trailblazer or an activist, inspiring others and leading to a change in some area. We have to be careful of being too headstrong with this mission however as it could lead us to override others or to not value their contribution.

## Eris in the Houses

We see the ethereal energies of the outer planets manifesting most clearly in our personal lives through their house position. The houses represent areas of our lives, and they focus a planet's energy and give it a playground.

### First House

With Eris in the 1st House, diversity consciousness is central to our world view. This is the house of self, and our mission is to trust ourselves. With this placement, we will be constantly evolving out of the current limits on our consciousness and opening ourselves to see beyond the finite bounds of our perception. This is the house of how others perceive us and, with this placement, we will do things differently from other people and will likely be seen either as a troublemaker, or as a truth-teller.

At the unconscious level, we are likely to argue back when challenged, whether this is appropriate or not, which is likely to antagonize people. And, at this level, our self-interest may make us greedy, and we could fall into workaholism, or we might try to win approval to get ahead.

When we are on the spiritual path, we can develop our self-awareness and free ourselves from addictions to success or status. At this level, we understand that we have to make the most of the spiritual growth opportunities in our lives and this gives us the strength and resourcefulness to do the work required.

Like British author, J.K. Rowling, known for promoting diversity and inclusivity in the Harry Potter series. Having faced multiple rejections from publishers before finding success with her debut novel, *Harry Potter and the Philosopher's Stone,* her resourcefulness is evident in her personal journey as a writer. Despite early financial struggles, she persevered and used her imagination and creativity to build a rich and intricate fictional world that captivated readers worldwide.

And, at the spiritually evolved level, we can see clearly without preconceptions, and we keep our body and mind in harmony so that health and happiness prevail. At this level we will have a personal sense of emergence. Through love and sympathy, we will be able to maintain the life of our spirit in times of crisis.

Like influential Indian spiritual leader and teacher, Yogi Bhajan, who introduced Kundalini Yoga to the Western world. He was the founder of the Healthy, Happy, Holy Organization, which promoted healthy living by emphasizing a balanced diet, regular exercise, and practices to enhance mental and emotional well-being. Kundalini Yoga is known for its dynamic and transformative nature, helping practitioners achieve physical strength, mental clarity, emotional balance, and a spiritual uplift.

**Second House**

With Eris in the 2nd House, we will have clear priorities regarding matters of love and money, as we understand that we can't take it with us and we apply our full resourcefulness in life. With this placement, we will have an alternative attitude towards wealth and material possessions, and may wish to live off the grid, understanding that 'sharing and caring' is key to our ability to provide for ourselves.

At the unconscious level, however, our greed and lack of spiritual regard for life could lead us to indulge in sensual pleasures and use our resources to try and dominate our social sphere. At this level, we are likely to be status oriented and may suffer from a lack of boundaries and a general sense of being forsaken, condemned, or abandoned. We might find ourselves speaking our mind at times when it is not appropriate and suffer consequences as a result.

Like American comedian, Roseanne Barr, known for her unique and often controversial comedic style. She has been lauded for her ability to push boundaries and tackle taboo subjects in her comedy. However, she has faced significant controversy due to her public statements, particularly through her use of social media, which have sometimes been criticized for being offensive, racist, or promoting conspiracy theories. These controversial statements have led to significant backlash and have had a negative impact on her career.

When we move onto the spiritual path, we can learn to keep our body and mind in harmony so that health and happiness prevail. As we do, we develop an inclusive world view, understanding that our sense of self-worth is dependent on the degree to which we are faithful to our values.

Like American author Ray Bradbury, whose science fiction spoke to broader societal issues, including censorship, social conformity, and the dangers of technology. His stories explored the consequences of neglecting the human spirit and the importance of maintaining a balance between technological advancements and emotional well-being. They frequently highlighted the value of individuality and the potential consequences of suppressing diverse perspectives.

At the spiritually evolved level, we can see clearly without preconceptions and can overcome crises through compassion. At this level, our diversity consciousness can provide safety, security, nourishment, or emotional support to those who may not know how to solve their problems themselves.

Like internationally renowned American intuitive, author, and public speaker, Linda Georgian, who approached her work as a professional intuitive as a way to educate and help people. Her book, *Your Guardian Angels,* was popular worldwide and published in several languages. She gave talks internationally in which she focused on health, spirituality, and personal empowerment. She also gave private intuitive readings to thousands of clients and consulted with law enforcement on missing persons cases.

**Third House**

With Eris in the 3rd House, the chaos in our minds brings ideas together when we give ourselves the freedom to think outside the box. With this placement, we will have a strong voice and can maintain our spirit steadily through all crises by being open to love and compassion.

At the unconscious level, however, we are likely to have a more superficial approach, overlooking details and arguing back when challenged, whether this is appropriate or not. At this level, we may lack a spiritual regard for life, and we may get caught in reactive thinking patterns. We need to learn to stop being fooled, or to stop fooling ourselves.

When we are on the spiritual path, we recognize the potency of our ideas and can adopt a sharing and caring approach to making connections. At this level, we may have a personal sense of emergence, understanding what is off balance in society and feel that it is our place to speak about this.

Like British novelist and Nobel laureate, Doris Lessing, who explored themes of inequality, racism, and the struggle for individual freedom and expression, all of which highlighted societal imbalances. Her books depict the struggles faced by people who challenge established norms and seek their own personal freedom, often questioning and critiquing oppressive systems and societal constraints in the process. She encourages her readers to examine the complexities of human existence and contemplate the possibilities for individual growth, liberation, and self-expression.

Then, at the spiritually evolved level, we value each person for who they are, accepting everything and neither comparing nor judging. At this level, our diversity consciousness enables us to be a thought leader, writing or speaking about our ideas.

Like prominent Tibetan Buddhist teacher and spiritual leader, Shamar Rinpoche, who emphasized the importance of meditation and mindfulness as powerful tools for achieving inner peace, clarity, and spiritual transformation. He guided his students to recognize and actualize their innate potential for awakening and spiritual growth, and provided teachings and practices related to the nature of mind, and which emphasize the inherent qualities of awareness and wisdom that lie within every individual.

**Fourth House**

With Eris in the 4th House, we are liberated from addictions to success or status and have the courage to break away from traditions and find ourselves. We may feel like we are the odd one out in the family and have childhood experiences of unequal power distribution causing problems in the home.

At the unconscious level, we may have a sense of being abandoned by family members and need to be careful of trying to win approval, or of developing co-dependent relationships.
We might also have a lack of boundaries, and as a result may feel used by others.

When we are on the spiritual path, however, we begin to see the karmic baggage we brought into this life and recognize how past conditions have contributed to our current problems. At this level, we can work through this karma, enabling us to keep our body and mind in harmony so that health and happiness prevail.

Russian chess grandmaster, world chess champion, and political activist, Garry Kasparov, exemplifies this karmic vision. He has frequently criticized the lingering effects of the Soviet legacy, emphasizing how the suppression of dissent, and the lack of democratic institutions have contributed to Russia's ongoing challenges. His diversity consciousness encouraged him to promote democratic reforms, hold leaders accountable for past actions, and foster a culture that prioritizes and protects individual freedoms.

And, at the spiritually evolved level, we understand our karmic lesson for this lifetime and have an ability to help those in need by providing safety, security, nourishment, or emotional support. At this level, we understand that non-judgmental attitudes help others to trust us.

Like well-known American psychic medium, Lisa Williams, who has dedicated her career to helping people connect with their loved ones who have passed away. She offers readings, workshops, and courses aimed at exploring spiritual growth and healing. Her approach is often described as compassionate and non-judgmental, creating a safe space for individuals seeking closure and guidance.

**Fifth House**

With Eris in the $5^{th}$ House, we will be a different drummer in our creative self-expression, inspiring others and provoking change by upsetting limited and antiquated structures of consciousness. With this placement, we feel the potency and inclusive nature of our life-force in our love and the way we raise our children.

At the unconscious level, however, we may not feel this potency and may instead feel forsaken or abandoned. As a result, we might throw ourselves into love affairs and the pursuit of pleasure, or into risk-taking and gambling, because of a lack of spiritual regard for life.

When we are on the spiritual path, however, we can maintain the life of the spirit steadily through all crises by staying open to love and sympathy. This encourages the development of an open heart, which is essential for personal transformation. At this level, we can see clearly without preconceptions, and we have the courage to take the spiritual risks necessary to grow in consciousness.

Like American occultist, author, and spiritual teacher, Dolores Ashcroft-Nowicki, who has studied Hermeticism, Kabbalah, Tarot, Alchemy, and other disciplines, and developed her own unique approach. She encourages direct experience of the divine, and the integration of esoteric principles into daily life. By fearlessly delving into esoteric practices and traditions, she has contributed to the expansion of esoteric knowledge and spiritual growth, and her openness to love and sympathy has enabled the sharing of these insights.

At the spiritually evolved level, we can transmute life into love, and value each person for who they truly are. At this level, we can keep our body and mind in harmony so that health and happiness prevail, and we might become a revered teacher.

Like renowned Indian spiritual teacher, Nityananda, who believed in the inherent divinity within all individuals and taught about self-realization and the unity of all beings. Understanding that true liberation comes from recognizing our essential nature beyond the limitations of the mind and body, he emphasized the importance of accepting oneself and others without judgment or discrimination.

**Sixth House**

With Eris in the 6th House, we have a potent way of responding to everyday crises, overcoming them through compassion. With this placement, we are likely to feel oppressed by the daily grind of normal jobs and may choose self-employment instead, where our maverick style is an advantage. This is also the house of wellness and health, and we are our own best health advisor when we listen to our inner guide and find a harmony in our daily rhythm.

At the unconscious level, however, we may not want to do the work of looking after ourselves, ignoring issues like personal hygiene until we become physically sick. Or we might find ourselves in a health crisis which is not managed well by our healthcare provider.

When we are on the spiritual path, we can adopt a more caretaking approach to our daily rhythm and feel a rise in vitality as a result. At this level, we might choose to have more agency by doing volunteer work, rather than paid work, understanding that helping others has its own rewards.

Like German spiritual teacher and author, Bo Yin Ra, who taught that by engaging in selfless acts, we can elevate our consciousness and experience a deeper connection with the Divine. In his books, he highlighted the importance of transcending self-centeredness and cultivating a genuine concern for the well-being of others. He believed that acts of selfless service contribute to the evolution of consciousness, fostering a sense of unity, love, and higher understanding.

At the spiritually evolved level, our diversity consciousness enables us to compassionately serve our community, providing safety, security, nourishment, and emotional support to those who may not know how to solve their problems themselves.

Like Dutch faith healer and counsellor, Greet Hofmans, who believed in the power of energy, and of the interconnectedness of mind, body, and spirit. She became known for her work providing emotional support and guidance to people, including members of the Dutch royal family. Her work emphasized the importance of addressing emotional well-being and understanding the mind, body, and spirit in a holistic way, to achieve health and harmony.

### Seventh House

With Eris in the 7th House, we have clear priorities regarding matters of love and money in our one-to-one relationships, and an ability to overcome crises through compassion. With this placement we can see through the details in our contracts and official documents.

At the unconscious level, however, we may have a superficial and status-oriented approach to our relationships and are likely to quarrel with our partners about issues of status or openness, and to argue back, whether this is appropriate or not. At this level, we are learning to stop being fooled, or to stop fooling ourselves, and we need to be careful of trying to win approval, or of forming co-dependent relationships. We may have a lack of boundaries and a feeling of being used, or there could be an uneven power dynamic in our relationships, which, either way, can lead to separation and lawsuits. The danger, when we are operating at the unconscious level, is that it's always easier to turn our truth-telling gaze on others and tell them what to do rather than focus it on ourselves.

Like the visionary founder of Apple Computers, Steve Jobs, who has a very close conjunction of Eris and the Moon in the 7th house. When he and his first long term partner and mother of his first child dropped acid together, he warned her that she should tell him, 'Not to put on airs' should he 'act out.' She didn't know what he meant at the time and it was only years later that she understood. He became a threatening monster when she became pregnant and denied being the father of their daughter despite a positive paternity test, then paid a pittance in child support while living the life of a millionaire. She visited him when their daughter was about thirteen years old and he and his new wife had a tiny baby boy. She recounts being outside his house, when, without warning, he blurted out the 'meanest, terrible comments' at her, about why she was such a total failure of a human being, only stopping when his wife yelled at him to stop.

When we are on the spiritual path, we can see ourselves and our partners more clearly and this diversity consciousness enables a more cooperative and sharing approach. At this level, our non-judgmental attitude is the key to our partners trusting us.

Like spiritual teacher and leader in the Siddha Yoga tradition, Gurumayi, whose teachings emphasize selfless service and foster a sense of unity and cooperation. She talks about the importance of nurturing positive, loving relationships with others. She encourages her followers to communicate openly, listen attentively, and work together to resolve conflicts in a compassionate and respectful manner. By promoting selfless service, unity, and cooperation, her teachings aim to create a sense of collective responsibility and shared well-being.

And, at the spiritually evolved level, we can transmute life into love, by valuing our partners in their naked splendor as we accept everything and neither compare nor judge them. At this level, our diversity consciousness fosters a community of like-minded people through our relationships.

Like prominent astrologer and writer, Alan Leo, who believed that astrology had a spiritual and philosophical dimension beyond mere fortune-telling. He emphasized using it as a tool for self-understanding, personal growth, and spiritual development. His approach aimed to empower individuals by helping them align with their true selves and life purpose. He founded the Astrological Lodge in London, providing a platform for education and fostering a community of like-minded individuals.

## Eighth House

With Eris in the 8th House, we understand the law of karma, and we get that we can't take it with us, so we need to apply our full resourcefulness in this life. This placement opens us to see beyond the finite bounds of our current perception and puts us in touch with deep truths.

At the unconscious level, however, we are more likely to have a sense of being forsaken, condemned, or abandoned. We may compensate for these feelings by acting in a greedy way, becoming a workaholic, or by getting addicted to success or status. At this level, inheritances, insurance payments and loans can be contentious areas. We might also have an interest in kinky sex. Or we could have a desire to sow chaos, as a way of empowering ourselves, but karma will always catch up with us and so this approach could also bring losses and debt.

When we are on the spiritual path, however, we will have a personal sense of emergence. At this level, we have open and clear priorities regarding matters of sex and joint resources, and we are in touch with deep truths and can bring them into our world, enriching and catalysing our collective energies in the process.

Like American author, astrologer, and spiritual teacher, Barbara Hand Clow, who has written extensively on astrology, mythology, and spiritual transformation. Her books delve into deep truths and provide spiritual insights, aiming to expand awareness and inspire a new understanding of the world. Through her books and teachings, she has sought to bridge the gap between spirituality and everyday life, encouraging us to explore our own spiritual paths and expand our consciousness.

At the spiritually evolved level, our deep truths will enliven the collective and inspire new faith. At this level, our diversity consciousness can sustain our spirit through all crises by maintaining an openness to love and sympathy.

Like the Indian philosopher, poet, and yogi, Sri Aurobindo, whose teachings emphasize the importance of love, compassion, and understanding in spiritual growth and the transformation of consciousness. He believed that love and sympathy are integral to human development and have the power to heal and uplift both individuals and society as a whole.

## Ninth House

With Eris in the 9th House, we will search for the meaning of things and have big thoughts and big ideas which will differ from the norm and are likely to be considered radical.
With this placement, we open to the light, and we finally get that we can't take it with us and instead apply our full resourcefulness in living fully.

At the unconscious level, however, we may instead feel oppressed by religion, rejecting spirituality and calling ourselves atheists. This could lead us to speak our mind, whether this is appropriate or not. A superficial and antagonistic approach is also likely to get us into confrontations in higher education settings, or when we are traveling. At this level, we may have a general lack of spiritual regard for life and instead have a sense of being forsaken, condemned, or abandoned.

This is exemplified by the work of American author, Stephen King, who writes about characters who experience the consequences of Eris at this unconscious level, and who is known for his contribution to the horror and suspense genres. He delves deep into the psyche of his characters, into their motivations and fears, making them feel authentic and multidimensional. His stories frequently explore themes such as fear, loss, trauma, and the darker aspects of human nature, and they combine ordinary, everyday settings with supernatural elements, creating a sense that horror can exist just beneath the surface of our normal lives.

Yet when we are on the spiritual path, we revel in the contentious debate of philosophical ideas, as these provide rich opportunities for our growth. Through this we can become a truth-teller, gaining a personal sense of emergence, and taking volatile ideas and baking them into new form through our work over time.

Like Russian American writer and philosopher, Ayn Rand, known for her individualistic and objectivist philosophy. She challenged conventional moral and ethical norms, advocating that we should each pursue our own values and reject altruism as morally superior. Her writings defended the rights of individuals to think for themselves, make choices based on reason, and pursue their own life goals without interference from the collective or government.

And, at the spiritually evolved level, we can see clearly without preconceptions, thus enabling us to develop a deep wisdom. As we shine this light into the world, people will be attracted by this wisdom, and we may become a revered teacher.

Like Indian philosopher and spiritual teacher, U.G. Krishnamurti, known for his radical and unconventional approach to enlightenment. His philosophy emphasizes the importance of direct and immediate experiential understanding, rather than relying on beliefs or concepts. He held that the mind was the source of all suffering, and that true freedom lies in the dissolution of the self-structure created by psychological thought patterns. He advocated for a natural and spontaneous way of living, free from the constructs and constraints of society and ideology, emphasizing the importance of self-inquiry and relying on our own direct experiences and observations. He taught that we need to be present in the here and now, rather than seeking enlightenment or spiritual progress in the future.

**Tenth House**

With Eris in the 10th House, we seek a social role that challenges the limiting and antiquated social structures and the prevailing collective consciousness that we find around us. With this placement, we have an ability to help those who have been left out, providing safety, security, nourishment, or emotional support, especially to those who may not know how to solve their problems themselves.

At the unconscious level, however, we might have a more status-oriented approach and become a workaholic, or we could react against authority figures, speaking out and achieving notoriety for our discordant views.

When we are on the spiritual path, we can see clearly without preconceptions, and we keep our body and mind in harmony so that health and happiness prevail. At this level, we realize that helping others has its own rewards and non-judgmental attitudes are the key to building trusted social foundations, so that we can all live in harmony.

Like American actress and comedian, Lily Tomlin, whose comedy often highlights the absurdities of societal norms and prejudices, urging audiences to question and challenge their own biases. Known for her versatility and comedic genius, she has masterfully portrayed characters from various backgrounds, often challenging stereotypes and shedding light on the complexities of human experiences. Her humor encourages self-reflection and introspection, reminding people not to take themselves too seriously and fostering an atmosphere of light-heartedness and acceptance.

At the spiritually evolved level, we can be liberated from addictions to success or status and can overcome social crises through compassion. We learn to transmute life into love, likely gaining recognition, community power, and prestige through this work. At this level, our diversity consciousness enables us to see the interconnectedness of everyone.

Like prominent American spiritual teacher and author, Ram Dass, known for his work on consciousness, mindfulness, and compassion. He encouraged his followers to cultivate a loving and compassionate attitude towards themselves and others, recognizing the inherent unity and interconnectedness of all beings. His book, *Be Here Now* introduced Eastern spiritual teachings to a Western audience in a relatable and accessible way. It combined memoir, philosophy, and practical guidance, as well as offering insights into the nature of the self, mindfulness practices, and the importance of living in the present moment.

**Eleventh House**

With Eris in the 11th House, we will seek out a group of like-minded friends who share our inclusive view of community. With this placement, we have big dreams and an ability to be non-judgmental and help those in need through support groups, or to reach out to those who may be excluded from these groups.

At the unconscious level, however, our need to belong might lead us to get involved with radical groups, or those with a chip on their shoulder. Or we might be excluded from groups altogether, which is likely to give us a feeling of being forsaken, condemned, or abandoned. At this level, we are learning to stop being fooled by our connections or to stop fooling ourselves.

When we move onto the spiritual path, however, we begin a process of self-realization and learn to see clearly without preconceptions. As our diversity consciousness develops, we can adopt a sharing and caring approach to our friendships. At this level, we seek out groups that help us keep our body and our mind in harmony, so we are healthy and happy.

Like American astronomer, astrophysicist, and cosmologist, Carl Sagan, who wrote about the interconnectedness of all life in his book, *Cosmos:*

*A Personal Voyage*. The book, and the accompanying television series, explored a wide range of scientific topics, including astronomy, cosmology, and biology, in an accessible and engaging manner. His series reached a massive audience and played a pivotal role in sparking interest in science worldwide.

Then, at the spiritually evolved level, we will be open to the promptings of love and sympathy and have a potent connection with our community. At this level, we can feel the currents in the collective consciousness, and our open heart enables us to maintain our contact with Spirit steadily through any crisis of consciousness that may arise.

Like well-known astrologer, author, and lecturer, Georgia Stathis, who specializes in financial astrology, analyzing the correlation between astrological patterns and economic trends. By connecting the patterns in the sky with everyday life, she helps people navigate challenges and make informed decisions in both personal and business areas. Her work in this area is highly regarded and she has provided valuable insights to individuals, investors, and businesses seeking guidance in financial matters.

**Twelfth House**

With Eris in the 12th House, our diversity consciousness enables us to see how our subconscious habit patterns exclude us from participating fully in our community. This enables us to work through these issues so we can apply our full resourcefulness in life.

At the unconscious level, however, we may sabotage our relationships by not working through this baggage, or we could suppress our discordant energy in an effort to conform.
At this level, we likely have a lack of spiritual regard for life, and may deceive ourselves or others, or undermine our efforts, by speaking out inappropriately. We need to be careful of trying to win approval, or of not being rigorous about our boundaries, because, either way, we could end up feeling used.

When we are on the spiritual path, we begin to understand that this baggage is karmic, and we learn to overcome it through compassion and adopting a less ego-centered approach. At this level, we are sensitive to the larger spiritual reality, and we might have an ability to help people find comfort, healing, and understanding through that contact.

Like renowned American medium, Arthur Ford, known for his compassionate approach in connecting with the spirit world. He would enter trance states, allowing a spirit known as "Fletcher" to speak through him and deliver messages to people seeking contact with their deceased loved ones. He gave many public demonstrations, gaining widespread attention and attracting large audiences. He was known for his ability to provide detailed and accurate information about the spirits he communicated with, often conveying highly specific details that were confirmed by the recipients of the messages.

And, at the spiritually evolved level, we have a deep connection with the spirit world and may experience revelatory events or miracles. At this level, we may have a powerful prophetic spiritual voice and an ability to channel the higher wisdom.

Like Ariel Guttman, a long-practicing astrologer and author who works within a richly spiritual framework rooted in mythology, Jungian psychology, and archetypal symbolism. Her work focuses on "the feminine" aspects of astrology, asteroid research, and connecting clients with mythological archetypes through her books and consulting practice. She is a mythic-spiritual teacher and scholar who believes the gods and goddesses of antiquity are living psychological and cosmic realities we can connect with through dreamwork, ritual, and astrological awareness.

## Workbook to Onboard Eris in Your Life

Work out where Eris is in your birth chart:

a. Go to www.astro.com and create a free account.
b. Then choose "Extended Chart Selection" under "Charts & Data" and put in your birth data.
c. On this data screen, at the bottom on the left under 'Additional Objects', you can choose to include the dwarfs, which are listed as Asteroids, and you do this by highlighting them. The dwarfs in this box are *Ceres, Eris, Ixion, Orcus, Makemake, Haumea, Quaoar, Sedna* & *Varuna.*
d. Then opposite this, in the box on the bottom right, add these numbers (**225088**, **120347**, **174567**, **541132**) to also include, Gonggong, Leleakuhonua, Varda & Salacia.
e. Click 'Show the Chart' to see it.
f. Then click 'Additional Tables' at the top left of the chart to get the table of positions and aspects.

Look up the house interpretation in this book for your house placement and see what resonates.

What does the Sabian Symbol for your Eris indicate to you? Search online for Dane Rudhyar's or Marc Edmund Jones's interpretations. (Remember to round up to find the right symbol, i.e. 22.04 = 23).

Next, understand how Eris interacts with the other planets in your chart by studying the aspects. I.e. – is Eris conjunct, opposite, trine, square or sextile any of your personal planets or points like Sun, Moon, Ascendant, Mercury, Venus, Ceres, Mars, Jupiter or Saturn? How about the transpersonal planets like Uranus, Neptune, Pluto, Ixion, Orcus, Salacia, Quaoar, Makemake, Gonggong, and Sedna?

Choose a significant moment of understanding in your life and look up the transits of Pluto and Saturn to your natal Eris on that date. You can find the list of where these two planets on this ephemeris: https://www.astro.com/swisseph/swepha_e.htm. And then check the Eris transits to your other natal planets. You can find the Eris ephemeris at this link: https://www.astro.com/swisseph/eris.htm.

Given what you've learned so far, write a couple of paragraphs on how can you best activate Eris in your life?

## Eris' Place in our New Firmament

The outer planets represent aspects of consciousness. We have become familiar with Uranus, Neptune and Pluto, and over the early years of this century we have discovered 12 new planets that offer us a rich feast of new consciousness. Let's look at each of these outer planets to put them in context.

As we embark on the spiritual path to make a larger sense out of the experiences of our personal lives, we start activating our Uranian and Neptunian energies and bring them into our consciousness. As we do, we begin to realize that the 'you can't take it with you" approach of the inner planets is actually a delusion.

**Uranus** brings intuitive flashes into our personal planet consciousness and begins to connect us with the collective consciousness, breaking through our Saturnian defenses to allow new impulses and connections. So, the discovery of Uranus enabled consciousness growth in our lives. We can look at Uranus as the higher octave of Mercury because he takes Mercury's ideas, communications and curiosity, and networks them at a higher spiritual level.

**Neptune** tunes us into the bigger picture and brings spiritual consciousness into our lives. He encourages us to search for a larger meaning for our personal experiences and teaches us about faith as a way of deepening consciousness. Neptune is traditionally considered to be the higher octave of Venus, where the inner planet's values and aesthetics are expressed at a more spiritual level through the imagination and psychic opening of Neptune.

Which brings us to dwarf planet **Pluto**, who is the start of the outer transpersonal planets. Here we must accept the limitations of the ego consciousness, let go of compulsions and unconscious constructs and accept that change is the only constant. Pluto is traditionally considered to be the higher octave of Mars.

The discovery of Pluto enabled the psychological understanding of our lives. This produced the shadow paradigm, where the darkness in our souls is seen to be buried in our unconscious, and the convenience of this is that we don't have to address it on a day-to-day basis. But we need to ditch Pluto's shadow paradigm to enable him and these other new energies consciously in our lives. As with all the other outer planets,

Pluto manifests differently depending on our level of consciousness, so what we have been calling his shadow is simply his manifestation when we are at personal planet consciousness.

As we get on the spiritual path, Pluto gives us an adaptability and resilience which enables us to mediate the transition occurring in our lives in each moment. And at the spiritually evolved level, we can transmute loneliness and separation into love and long-term relationships and effect a regeneration in our lives.

Pluto now has two new brothers who share his orbit and his angle to the ecliptic. They also share his gravitational resonance with Neptune, as all three do two orbits of the Sun, to every three of Neptune's. These brothers are however polar opposites.

The first is **Ixion**, who encourages us to be a passionate, but lawless, follower of our heart, or loins, depending on our consciousness level. He's always asking the question: 'are the rules we're playing by the right ones?' And he does this by pushing the boundaries and asking for forgiveness afterwards, rather than permission before. As we develop a spiritual approach, we can learn to honor the bad girl or bad boy energy inside us and follow our heart. At this level Ixion encourages us to be an independent and unique expression of ourselves, while being sensitive to the unspoken agreements in our relationships, so we know how far we can go.

The second is Pluto's straight-talking brother, **Orcus**, our new karmic consciousness. He is the master of integrity at the highest level, but he also encourages us to engage in double-talk and deception at the personal planet level. Yet as we develop spiritually, he gives us a self-sufficiency that will nourish us through the long and difficult work that we sometimes find necessary, plus a capacity to deal with the shadow side of our lives. At this level we become accountable for our deeds and actions. We learn to align with a spiritual creed and understand the karmic process of life. And, at the highest level, we gain the shamanic ability to transmute shadow into light.

Next, we have **Salacia**, our new higher-love consciousness, who gives us a self-protective quality that helps us weather both the physical and the psychic storms in our lives. She can give us the power to foresee opportunities and find the appropriate time to embrace them. She enables us to take a leap of faith, especially when we know we are going to be profoundly transformed by the experience. At the personal planet level there can be erotic fascination or interest, and we might engage in socially unacceptable, even illicit, sexual activity. As we develop spiritually, she brings a light-heartedness that enables our psychic intimacy with others and can bring popularity. At the highest level, Salacia is about bringing true love into our lives and empowering us spiritually.

Then we have **Varuna**, our new mastery consciousness, who is the higher octave of Saturn. Where Saturn rules by control and through laws and restriction, Varuna has a natural sovereignty, but we have to claim this through action. Sovereignty is a dance between our intention and the collective psyche. We have to claim it and at the same time others have to agree to give it to us. We start this process by stepping forth in some way and saying, 'I can do this'. And then we have to keep doing it over time. And, when we do, we gain support and notability for this work. Once we are on the spiritual path, Varuna teaches us to stand in the centre of our lives and own the results of our dance of karma and dharma. And at the top level we find a sovereignty and a mastery which is built from experience and supported by a like-minded community.

As we move further out from the Sun, we find **Haumea**, our new unity consciousness, who is a creation deity of the Hawaiian people. She is both an earth goddess and a fire goddess, and she represents regeneration and rebirth. She is the higher octave of Neptune, turning his psychic opening into real psychic connection. At the personal planet level, however, this can manifest as a lack of connection, a sort of spiritual alienation. As we develop spiritually, she provides a link with the oneness of humanity, with the magic of being alive. So, she represents a direct link with the soul level when we can open ourselves to it, and, as we deepen this connection to Source, we learn to facilitate a constant psychic renewal in our own lives and in the lives of others.

Just beyond Haumea, we have our first non-gendered planet, **Quaoar**, our new spirit consciousness. Quaoar is the creation deity of the Tongva people, who are indigenous to Los Angeles. Quaoar sings and dances the world into existence, so this planet talks about a practice of bringing spirit into matter. Singing and dancing are practices that bring spirit into matter, and so are yoga, meditation, walking in the woods, and many other things. Anything can be a practice to bring spirit into our lives. We can look at Quaoar as the higher octave of Jupiter. Where Jupiter is a sort of dumb luck, Quaoar turns each moment into a dynamic meditation where we can see the opportunities and act on them in real time, so Quaoar is like smart luck.

Our next planet is **Makemake**, opening us to the new richness of systems consciousness, which gives us a worldview built from our experience, and a view of our place in that world. He is a spiritual trickster, enabling us to innovate and to play with the area of life signified by his position in our natal chart. He encourages us to see ourselves as an organic whole, as well as a member of a team. We can look at him as the higher octave of Uranus, lifting Uranus' intuition into a rich understanding of life. At the personal planet level, we might use this rich intuitive understanding to hide in plain sight, to blend into the background as a safety mechanism. As we develop spiritually however, he calls spiritual nourishment into our lives and gives us a devotional focus bordering on genius.

Then we have **Varda**, our new inspiration consciousness. Varda is the much-loved Elven goddess from *The Lord of the Rings*, who kindled the starlight. She enables us to win our battles with the dark forces through hope and inspiration, and she can lead us through a transition to a new state of being. She's all about finding the light in our lives or shining our light in the world. So, she enables us to navigate the "dark night of the soul" or any other "dark" confusing time. She trains us to be more objective, more careful, more aware of whole situations — and less impulsive and intent upon side issues. And she supports us to walk away from previous betrayals and associations and encourages us to look towards new horizons and start afresh elsewhere.

This is followed by **Gonggong**, our new empathic consciousness, who encourages us to participate in the marketplace of life. He is an psychic wizard at the highest level, enabling us to feel inside other people and walk a mile in their shoes. We have to get out of our own emotions to empathize with others however, so at the personal planet level, he can be a bit of an enfant terrible, encouraging us to be emotionally self-indulgent and to lash out in an attempt to get our own way. As we develop spiritually, we understand that we live in a symbiotic relationship with others, and that our divine work is to let go of our own base emotions so we can be sensitive to the emotional community in which we are nestled and open to the empathic support of others. This empathy allows us to motivate others from the inside, to combine our energies and lift the spiritual vibe.

Next, we have **Eris**, our new diversity consciousness, who is the warrior sister of Mars in myth. And we know that Pluto is the higher octave of Mars, so Eris is the higher octave of Pluto. She shines her fierce grace on everything in our lives, seeking inclusion and validation for all the disparate facets of our psyche. At the personal planet level, she encourages us to engage in discord and strife, so we learn to stop fooling ourselves, or stop being fooled. But as we adopt a more spiritual approach, she enables us to see clearly without preconceptions and keep our body and mind in harmony so that health and happiness prevail. And at the highest level she is a spirit-guide, transmuting life into love.

Then we make a big jump to **Sedna**, our new soul consciousness, who has an orbit of over eleven thousand years. Sedna is always trying to get us onto the spiritual path. She represents *Our Soul's Path of Destiny* because, if we accept that our soul incarnates over a number of lifetimes and that it has a purpose to grow through these incarnations, then in this life, that purpose is shown by the Sedna placement. She is always trying to get us onto the spiritual path, and when we are unconscious of her energy, she sends us transcendent crises to help us let go of our old consciousness framework and transcend to a new one. As we step up to do the soul-based work that we are here to do, we move through a fated transcendence to a more transpersonal consciousness. We learn to embrace our spiritual destiny and joyfully do what our soul wants to do, and this brings us transcendent peace and the ability to allow love and harmony, and nurture abundance.

And finally, we come to **Leleakuhonua**, our new multi-dimensional consciousness, who talks of the soul growth mission that we are all on together. Leleakuhonua has an orbit 5 times as large as Sedna, so it steps Sedna's soul consciousness up to become a unified soul-field, where, at the top level, we can see our soul reflected in the other souls in our lives. This planet teaches us to be both independent and interdependent at the same time, and it talks about the huge missions we have to undertake to make a change in our lives so that we can better sustain ourselves. This planet gives us extrasensory abilities, where we can 'read the field' on a level which is far greater than just picking up the sensory cues, and this includes precognition. Our soul knows it's journey and the more we can tap into our higher selves and be sensitive to the signals from our soulmates, the better we will be able to orient ourselves on our big collective soul-growth mission.

## Dwarf Planets as Higher Octaves

Here is a framework of higher octaves to help us understand several of the dwarf planets. A higher octave expresses an inner planet energy at a more spiritual level and so gives us one way to understand these new bodies.

But Dane Rudhyar reminds us in this quote from Horoscope Magazine, that the higher octaves also act on the lower octaves to repolarize and transform them.

> *When Uranus, Neptune and Pluto are considered as "higher" expressions of such planets as Mercury, Venus and Mars... the closer planets are seen to represent a "lower octave" of biological-personal functions or energies; the more remote ones, beyond Saturn, a "higher octave" constituted of more transcendent and "spiritual" activities or qualities of being.*
>
> *There is some truth, no doubt, in such statements if one restricts oneself to a consideration of only the external events of a person's life. The "illuminations" which Uranus may bring to the consciousness that is not frozen into Saturnian rigidity can inspire and transform the Mercury mind. The compassion and inclusiveness which are characteristic of Neptune do act directly — if allowed by Saturn so to act—upon the sense of value and the feeling-judgments represented by Venus. The power of inescapable destiny and total surrender to a cause, which defines essentially Pluto's operations, do transform — if allowed to do so — the strictly personal initiative of Mars.*
>
> *But the essential fact is that the activities of Uranus, Neptune and Pluto run counter to the normal functions of Mercury, Venus and Mars. The former are not just personal activities of a "higher" kind; they are activities meant to disturb and transform — indeed, utterly to repolarize and reorient those of Mercury, Venus and Mars.*[9]

So, with that in mind, here is a higher octave framework for some of our new dwarf planets. (The planets in bold are dwarf planets).

9 https://www.khaldea.com/rudhyar/astroarticles/planetaryoctaves.php

**Sedna** - **Ceres** - Moon
**Haumea** – Neptune – Venus
**Makemake** – Uranus – Mercury
**Eris** – **Pluto** – Mars
**Quaoar** – Jupiter
**Varuna** - Saturn

We can think of **Sedna** as the higher octave of **Ceres**, who is our newly reclassified inner dwarf planet. Ceres is our ability to love and be loved. At both a basic level and in the bigger sense of the word, she represents what we need to feed and nourish ourselves. And we can think of Ceres as the higher octave of the Moon. The Moon is our emotional center, mediating our survival moment to moment, and Ceres mediates our survival over time. Sedna steps this heart-centered energy all the way out to the new limit of our solar system, so she talks of our survival over lifetimes. Here we learn to let go of the physical realm and allow transcendence to a new holistic spiritual consciousness where we can allow love and harmony, and nurture abundance.

We can look at **Makemake** as the higher octave of Uranus, which in modern astrology is the higher octave of Mercury. Makemake gives Uranus's intuitive impulses meaning and context, which transforms our understanding of his unexpected ways. And Uranus's lateral web gives Mercury's detail an energetic network to organize and connect his information. All three planets are tricksters, and Makemake is a spiritual trickster who allows us to experiment with the area of life signified by his position in our chart.

We can think of **Haumea** as the higher octave of Neptune, where Neptune's psychic opening has the potential to blossom into real psychic connection with Haumea, a connection to the soul level. Neptune is traditionally considered to be the higher octave of Venus, echoing her values and aesthetics at a higher spiritual level. We see a love of beauty and a belief in values in all three of these bodies.

In mythology **Eris** is the warrior sister of Mars, and in our lives, where Mars is fighting mundane battles, Eris' challenge is on a more esoteric level. In modern astrology **Pluto** is considered to be the higher octave of Mars, so we can look at Eris as the higher octave of Pluto. She steps up his transformative energy to a fierce grace through which everything in our lives is opened to the light and can be transmuted into love.

We can look at **Quaoar** as the higher octave of Jupiter. Both planets talk of expansion and of new possibilities, but where Jupiter expands through a mix of luck and a hunger for more, Quaoar repolarizes Jupiter so we can see the new opportunities and deftly take the appropriate action to enable the expansion that is possible in each moment. Where Jupiter is a sort of dumb luck, Quaoar turns each moment into a dynamic meditation, where we can see the opportunities and act on them in real time. So, Quaoar is like smart luck.

And we can think of **Varuna** as the higher octave of Saturn. Both are supreme rulers, but where Saturn limits, controls, and structures, Varuna transmutes this energy into self-sufficient mastery. However, like Saturn, Varuna can place restrictions on us if we are not being true to ourselves or honest with others, but these dissipate when we forgive and align with Spirit.

### **Gonggong** – **Salacia** – Mars/Venus

We look at **Gonggong** as being the higher octave of **Salacia**, who we see as the higher octave of Venus and Mars combined. If there was a planet that combined Venus and Mars it would be all about relationship and sexuality, and Salacia steps that up to a psychic one-to-one contact, while Gonggong steps that up even further to an empathic contact with an ability to channel psychic and emotional energy.

### **Ixion – Pluto - Orcus**

And finally, Pluto now has two new brothers who share his orbit as well as his angle to the ecliptic. All three are at the same octave level. The two brothers are, however, polar opposites. The first is the seeker consciousness of **Ixion**, who enables us to develop our authenticity. While the second, **Orcus**, opens us to karmic consciousness, teaching us to align with a spiritual creed and understand the karmic process of life.

## Dwarf Planet University

The information in this book comes out of research at the Dwarf Planet University, where we are pioneering the astrological exploration of the Kuiper Belt. The dwarf planets speak of new aspects of consciousness that are arising in our lives, and we offer 6-week courses to on-board each of them.

The courses explore the planets in our personal chart and the charts of the other class members. We look at the house placement and the aspects and research our transits, as we understand how to on-board each aspect of consciousness.

The course format mixes webinars, blog-posted assignments and live Zoom Q&As, so you can attend from anywhere in the world. We start with a live Welcome Q&A and we explore the House position in the first fortnight, the aspects in the second and transits in the third. Each fortnight includes an instructional webinar, an investigative assignment based on your personal chart and a live 2 hour Zoom Q&A session.

Assignments are posted on a private forum so we can learn from, and comment on, posts from our fellow course members. And the live Q&A sessions are recorded so we can pick up classes we miss.

The students on our courses range from beginners to very experienced astrologers, and it is this range that is the source of the vibrant class culture. What students love is the community sharing that occurs, through the blog-posted assignments and live Zoom Q&As, which gives a good picture of how these new planets act similarly, and yet diversely, in each of our lives.

We offer a Dwarf Planet Astrology Diploma on completion of any 8 of our 13 courses, but you are also welcome to do courses singly and in any order. All the courses have a mix of ongoing and casual students, which provides a creative cross pollination of experience levels.

**What Students Say:**

*I highly recommend the Dwarf Planets Course for the insights and the amount of new information and perspective gathered. Alan's teaching inspires one and brings new light and spiritual understanding to charts (certainly to mine). His humor and friendly approach made the seminars very enjoyable, yet profound.*

Elisabetta Quintiliani - Italy

*Alan Clay's sensitive, cutting edge wisdom and the community sharing make the classes on the Dwarf Planets compelling and profound. They are as much an exploration as a revelation. Not only mentally stimulating, they are a deep dive into each of our psyche and growth experience. I love them and am looking forward to more.*

Karen La Puma, Astrologer, Counsellor, Speaker

*I'm very grateful for Alan Clay's insightfully powerful dwarf planet courses. He offers a supportive and welcoming class environment that encourages learning and processing the deep new consciousness of these planets. I totally recommend engaging with this outer realm of alchemy into our inner self!*

Sue Rose Minahan, Evolutionary Post-Modern Astrologer

*What Alan Clay has created with the Dwarf Planet University is nothing short of genius. His in-depth knowledge and amazing teaching style are unique and what the astrological world has been waiting for. I'm so enjoying learning about our far-reaching dwarf planets amongst a galaxy of friendly, intelligent student astrologers from all over the universe, logging on at their differing time zones.*

Eileen Richardson, UK.

*Alan Clay's work has transformed my thinking—about my chart, about my practice—even about astrology itself. Alan is a born teacher.*

Ariel Harper Nave, Canada

*I absolutely loved the class! As a first-time student of astrology, I can honestly say that aside from Alan (a wonderful teacher and guide), every one of the students in the class was a teacher for me. I learned so much and can't wait for the next class to begin. -*

Mary Anne Pitt, USA

*Who would have thought that studying the dwarf planets would lead to such an expansive awareness of my soul's journey? For this, I am very grateful. The style and structure of Alan's teaching provides the group with a very warm, safe and informative space in which to learn. I love being part of the group. Thank you, Alan.*

Marian Ryan, Energy Therapist, Author, Teacher, UK

*As one returning to astrological study after decades away, I find Alan's instruction fun and informative, and the classroom format a gift of shared learning for everyone participating. Alan has created a safe and supportive space where anyone, at any level of knowledge, can thrive and shine. His obvious love of this work illuminates its presentation. I echo the comments of others, "Best astrology classes ever!"*

Nalini MacNab, USA

"I have been sensing a reciprocity in my study of the dwarf planets. As I shift focus and embrace each of their unique energies, I am in turn rewarded by a richer understanding of myself and the world in which we live."

Alison Glennie, Ireland

## Meet the Writers

New Zealander **Alan Clay** is transpersonal astrologer, specialising in the outer planets, and inspired by the work of Dane Rudhyar. Over the years this has broadened into a study of the new dwarf planets, and today he is one of the Kuiper Belt's astrological pioneers.

Alan worked for many years internationally as a clown and a clown teacher, which he describes as being a big research into people and what makes us human. And he combined this with consulting astrology work to explore the depths or our psyche.

He is well known for his clown textbook, *Angels Can Fly*, which includes a mix of clown theory, workshop and street exercises, anecdotes from 20 international clowns, and fictional stories following the adventures of 10 street clowns.

He is also the writer and director of an award winning romantic comedy film, *Courting Chaos*, in which a Beverly Hills girl falls for a Venice Beach street clown called Chaos, and she must overcome her inhibitions and become a clown herself for the relationship to survive.

His novel, *Believers in Love*, tells the story of a father and daughter team of sand-sculptors, who embark on a crazy adventure from Bondi Beach to a magic mountain in New Zealand, exploring the transient nature of art and life, to discover that dreams are real. Reviewers called it *"A book about love, laughter and life. Not just a story, this is an exploration of emotion and philosophy. A novel of journey and self-discovery."*

Alan's first astrology book, *Sedna Consciousness, the Soul's Path of Destiny* was launched at United Astrology Conference 2018 in Chicago. It is the ultimate reference on the new outer limit of our solar system, the planet Sedna. The book includes aspect interpretations with all the traditional planets, as well as all the new dwarf planets.

Following several years of teaching dwarf planet astrology courses online, Alan founded the Dwarf Planet University under the Jupiter/ Saturn conjunction in 2000. Since then he has developed all the course material that is used by students at the Uni, and he leads the fortnightly live Zoom Q&As. He still works as a consulting astrologer and is available for chart readings by Zoom.

In 2024 Alan published *New Stars for a New Era: A Consciousness Workbook for our 10 New Planets*. This book includes chapters on Ixion, Orcus, Salacia, Varuna, Haumea, Quaoar, Makemake, Gonggong, Eris and Sedna.

*"Alan Clay has written a comprehensive book on the newly discovered dwarf planets, exploring everything from their mythology to practical application. More than just reading about these celestial bodies, Alan shows us how to work with their energies and incorporate them into our lives. Best of all, the book is accessible to both seasoned astrologers and novices eager to gain an understanding of the emergence of new consciousnesses in our world. A strong recommendation for this groundbreaking book."*

Armand Diaz, from a review in the NCGR Memberletter

**Melissa Elvira Billington** is the child of a healer and a physicist, conceived in a conscientious objector's community in Nova Scotia but born in Virginia and raised in the Northeastern US. She worked in the arts in Santa Fe, Boise, and New York City before heading to India in 1999 for the last full solar eclipse of the last millennium.

As the stars would have it, she has lived and worked as an artist and yoga teacher in India, Barbados, Puerto Rico, New Zealand, and now Australia. She has studied dwarf planet astrology with Alan for seven years and worked as an assistant teacher at the Dwarf Planet Uni for the last four.

Here is her first spiritual work, age 7, fresh from the ashram:

*Inner and Outer space*
*is a wondrous place*
*to be at peace with yourself.*

*Love is the peace of mind*
*that binds us together*
*in outer and inner space as one.*

In 2023 the Dwarf Planet University started publishing a series of textbooks on the new planets which were co-written by Melissa and Alan. *The Astrology of Haumea, Neptune's Higher Octave* was released in May, and *The Astrology of Makemake, Uranus' Higher Octave* in October. This is the third book in the series.

www.ingramcontent.com/pod-product-compliance
Lightning Source LLC
LaVergne TN
LVHW052347100826
845147LV00012B/778

* 9 7 8 0 6 4 5 8 0 3 3 4 1 *